CROP

 a beginner's guide

HUGH MANISTRE

Hodder & Stoughton

A MEMBER OF THE HODDER HEADLINE GROUP

For M–W

Acknowledgements

I would like to acknowledge the contributions of Teresa and Helen
for getting me started; Jim, Kelvin and the McSweeneys for PC help;
Mark and Tim Butler, agricultural consultants; Nikki M. and
Circular Forum 91–92; Paul Fuller, Peter Rendall, George Bishop;
Deidre and Simon for renting me the cottage I wrote this in, and the
girls for putting up with me when I did.

Orders: please contact Bookpoint Ltd, 39 Milton Park, Abingdon, Oxon OX14 4TD.
Telephone: (44) 01235 400414, Fax: (44) 01235 400454. Lines are open from
9.00–6.00, Monday to Saturday, with a 24-hour message answering service. Email
address: orders@bookpoint.co.uk

British Library Cataloguing in Publication Data
A catalogue record for this title is available from The British Library

ISBN 0 340 74753 6

First published 1999
Impression number 10 9 8 7 6 5 4 3 2 1
Year   2005 2004 2003 2002 2001 2000 1999

Typeset by Transet Limited, Coventry, England.
Printed in Great Britain for Hodder & Stoughton Educational, a division of Hodder
Headline plc, 338 Euston Road, London NW1 3BH by Cox and Wyman Limited,
Reading, Berks.

CONTENTS

INTRODUCTION 1

Chapter 1   WHAT IS A CROP CIRCLE?   2

Characteristics of the circles 3
Development and progression 3
Terminology 5

Chapter 2   EARLY HISTORY OF THE CIRCLES 7

Early research 7
Eye-witness and historical accounts 8
Escalation of numbers and interest 10

Chapter 3   THE GOLDEN AGE 1989–91   14

Surveillance attempts 14
Design developments 15
1990: The appearance of the pictograms 16
New surveillance attempts 18
The Cerealogist 20
1991 21

Chapter 4   THEORIES AND EXPLANATIONS 28

Nature traditions 28
Meteorological theories 30
Supernatural explanations 32
Hoax explanations 37

Chapter 5   SCIENCE AND THE CIRCLES   40

Plasma research 40
Crop and soil research 41

Testing human capabilities   44
Evaluating the research   45

ChApTER 6   The New Age, the pARANORMAL and the cIRcLES   49

Dowsing   49
New Age ideology   51
Channelling and paranormal events   52
Spiritual ideas   54

ChApTER 7   hoAx! The cIRcLEMAKERS   56

Early hoaxes   56
Development of hoax theory   57
Doug and Dave   59
Other circlemakers   61

ChApTER 8   PARANOIA AND cONSPIRAcy   65

Government involvement?   65
Disinformation   67

ChApTER 9   PSychOLOGY AND the cIRcLES   71

The appeal of the circles   71
Effects on people   73
Human–environmental interactions   75
Psychology of the circlemakers   77

ChApTER 10   The cIRcLES wORLDwIDE   80

Australia   80
Canada   81
United States   81
Japan   82
Europe   82

ChApTER 11   PuTTING IT ALL TOGEThER   84

FuRThER READING AND RESOuRcES   88

INTRODUCTION

Since 1980, when the first reports began circulating, each year has brought fresh developments to the mystery of the crop circles. Although their public profile has waned since its height between 1989 and 1991, the circles have not gone away and have, if anything, become more spectacular and beautiful in recent seasons.

The circles have provided regular copy for newspapers during the summer 'silly season', when there is little political news, people are on holiday and hard news is scarce. Traditionally, editors look for stories in a humorous, light-hearted vein and their treatment of the circles, which conveniently appear at this time of the year, consequently tends towards the frivolous. 'Little green men' will often be mentioned, along with the inevitable 'boffins'. But to crop circle researchers, circles are anything but frivolous: people have abandoned jobs in pursuit of them! The subject has its own journals, societies and ongoing research projects, ranging from laboratory science to bizarre field experiments.

This book traces the history and development of the circles, from the earliest accounts and eye-witness reports, to the present. Along the way we will encounter UFOs, mystics, visionaries, dowsers and sceptics and, as the evidence unfolds, you will be able to arrive at your own conclusions about the meaning and explanation of the circles.

Each chapter contains brief practical suggestions which can serve as a framework for your own research. You may find, as I did, that this leads you into other related fields of knowledge and interest.

WHAT IS A CROP CIRCLE?

In their simplest form crop circles appear as, roughly circular markings in grass, or crops such as wheat, barley and oilseed rape. On the ground, the crop is seen to be pressed flat, with a distinctive swirled pattern, ending with a sharply defined edge, beyond which the standing crop is unaffected. The spiral pattern can be either clockwise or anti-clockwise and, when viewed from above, appears strikingly beautiful, as if stamped or printed into the crop.

A basic crop circle

Characteristics of the circles

Various design characteristics can be described:

- **Apparent, but not perfect, circularity**
  When measured, the 'circle' is found to tend towards an ellipse.
- **Sharply defined perimeter**
  This has been described as a 'cookie cutter' effect, as if the circle has been cut with a huge biscuit cutter.
- **Stems laid almost flat to the ground**
  Often said to be 'bent but not broken'. When fresh (e.g. before visitors have trampled it) the crop appears in 'bundles', bent right over, almost horizontal.
- **Swirled, spiralling, veined or banded appearance to the flattened stems**
  A sense of 'flow'.
- **'Precision' effects**
  Rows of single stems left standing within the formation.
- **Weaving, interlaced lays**
  Sections of the formation where there are underlying bands, often at 'junctions'.
- **Precise positioning within the field**
  - aligned to the tramlines
  - remote from the tramlines
  - not crossing field boundaries.

Sightings of crop circles have been reported from countries around the world, but it has been those found in the English counties of Hampshire and Wiltshire which have received most attention.

Development and progression

As researchers began to accumulate data over a number of years, two apparent trends were noted. Firstly, the number of circles discovered each year increased and, secondly, the design complexity appeared to show evolution.

3

Estimates vary as to the numbers logged each year, but it is accepted that between 1980 and 1991 there was an increase each year, beyond that accounted for by increased observation of the landscape.

A gradual progression has occurred, beginning with single circles, then multiple circles in formation; doubles, triples and quintuplets, then single and double rings, then avenues connecting circles. Over time a bewildering variety of shapes has been recorded, including triangles, spirals, ellipses, with the list increasing each season.

It has been this sense of progression, with the underlying implication of intelligent design, that has fuelled public fascination with the circles.

Types of crop

Circles have been found in a variety of crops and there are also reports of markings in snow and sand. The most common crops in which circles appear in the United Kingdom are wheat and barley, but they can also occur in grass, oil seed rape and oats. Outside the United Kingdom circles have been reported in rice, reed beds, spinach and maize.

Farming practice

Arable farms grow cereals for a number of uses, predominantly bread, animal feeds, biscuits and brewing. Smaller quantities are grown for seed. Different varieties of wheat, barley and other crops will be chosen for different purposes. Wheat suitable for milling or barley suitable for malting (for brewing) attract a premium, but yield less per acre.

Other than organically grown crops (currently accounting for only 1 per cent of all agriculture in the United Kingdom), cereals will be sprayed with a variety of chemicals through their growing cycle. The regular passage of the tractor in the field is allowed by planting with regular gaps. These will be determined by the width of the spraying arm, so that an arm of 16 metres will give tramlines at that width.

A farmer will, probably, harvest the flattened crop in a circle formation, by lowering the height of the cut. If the crop was flattened early in the season, the grain will not develop properly as it will not receive sufficient light. The crop is at its most vulnerable just after flowering, when the developing seed head has a lot of moisture, the stem is bendy and the leaves of the plant will hold water, making the plant heavier. Heavy winds and rain at this time can cause substantial damage. A crop flattened early in the season will try to regain a vertical position, through the phototropic response of turning towards the light. Later in the year, it will stay flattened.

In the United Kingdom, the first circles of the year usually appear in oilseed rape, followed by barley and then wheat. The 'season' runs from late April through to harvest, generally from July to September.

Terminology

Like all specialist subjects, the circles have acquired a language of their own. The following list explains some of the commonly used terms:

- **Aerial phenomena**, such as lights in the sky, are seen in association with the circles.
- **Banding** refers to the pattern that appears as bunches of stems are swept into noticeable 'ribs'.
- **Corn circles** or **crop circles** describe the general phenomenon, or the simplest markings.
- **Croppies** are those who are obsessed with the circles.
- **Dowsable traces**, detectable with dowsing rods or a pendulum, might be left behind after the circle forms.
- **Energies** are said to cause or remain in the formations.
- **Flow** is the term used to describe the directional sense of the stems. Counter-flows describe stems lying in a direction different from the surface flow.
- **Gap-seeking** occurs where a bundle of stems spills into the tramlines left by tractor wheels.

- **Grapeshot** are small or tiny circles scattered at random round the main circles.
- **Lay** is used to describe the pattern of the flattened crop, which might be seen to be clockwise or anti-clockwise, perhaps with spiral or concentric veining.
- **Pictograms** describe more complex formations.
- **Rings** are narrow, or wide circular pathways around a central circle.
- **Satellite** is used to describe small circles arranged around a larger one.

Spread of interest worldwide

It may be that, in previous ages, crop circles were seen only by the farmers when they harvested their fields. Nowadays, fields are regularly overflown by aircraft and this, together with the public's insatiable appetite for novelty, have combined to inflate interest in the circles. This reached a peak in 1991, but since then the circles have entered the visual vocabulary, appearing in advertisements, on album covers, in television shows and generally achieving an acceptance alongside the usual range of 'paranormal' phenomena.

Practice

Over the course of a season, observe the growth of cereal crops. Notice the tramline patterns. Identify the kind of crop; wheat, barley, oil seed rape, etc. Observe the changes in appearance as the crop matures.

EARLY HISTORY
OF THE CIRCLES

EARLY RESEARCH

*In many ways the early history of the circles belongs to the UFO
community. Reports of circular markings have been investigated by
UFO researchers on a number of occasions prior to the growth of
interest in the 1980s, and have often been interpreted as UFO landing
sites. Particularly well-known cases include markings in a spinach
patch in France in 1954, circles at Warminster in the United Kingdom
and circles found in a reed bed in Tully, Australia in 1966. A witness
at the site reported seeing a 'UFO' take off, leaving a patch of uprooted
and scattered reeds, in a circular shape, which came to be known as a
UFO nest.*

It was a UFO researcher who carried out the first recorded survey of
a circle in the United Kingdom. In August 1980, the *Wiltshire Times*
reported a formation of three circles which had appeared near
Westbury, below one of the white horses which are carved in chalk
and scattered on hillsides in this region. Ian Mryzyglod investigated
the circles and concluded that they were not 'landing marks' of a
UFO. He then contacted Dr Terence Meaden, an atmospheric
physicist who suggested that the probable cause was a summer
whirlwind. Mryzyglod arranged for samples of the affected crop to be
tested at Bristol University, where no abnormalities were detected.

In the next few years, as circles continued to be discovered, researchers
began to accumulate data and older records came to light. These early
records assumed greater importance when the subject later became
surrounded in controversy.

Eye-witness and historical accounts

Dr Meaden published eye-witness accounts of circles forming in the United Kingdom, one of which dated from the 1930s (see Further Reading). The witness, Katherine Skin, recalled seeing two circles form on a hot August day in 1934 in Cambridgeshire. Their appearance was preceded by a whirlwind in which stalks, seeds and dust were visible. Inside the circle she saw that some stalks had been plaited. Another witness described an event in South Wales, dating from the 1940s, and Meaden also wrote of a double ring photographed in 1960, in Gloucestershire. This was reported in the *Evesham Journal* and attracted quite a number of visitors.

Andrews and Delgado (see Further Reading) quote a farmer, Simon Brown, recalling circles on his farm at Headbourne Worthy almost every year since 1958. Paul Fuller, in *The Crop Watcher 14*, lists a number of other 'early' circles, including reports from the Netherlands, Canada, France, Australia, New Zealand, Sweden, Turkey and the United States. The list runs to some 78 items, mainly rings, simple circles or elipses and multiple circles.

Perhaps the most famous example was published by Bob Rickard, who came across a woodcut from 1678, in a book on folklore, *Bygone Hertfordshire* showing a 'Mowing Devil' at work, creating what looks like a primitive crop circle. The text tells how a farmer, who was in dispute with his farm hand over the price of the job, swore he would rather the devil cut the crop. The next night a fiery light was observed in the field and the crop was later found to be cut in precise circles. Although this has been disputed as a representation of the phenomenon we recognize now (mainly because of the description of the crop as cut), it seems beyond doubt that the circles have been occurring for many years.

Further evidence of this has been researched by Mark Haywood, following Bob Rickard's lead, and comes from a 1686 book by Robert

Plot, an Oxford professor. In *The Natural History of Staffordshire* he describes his investigations of 'rings in grass ... which they commonly call fairy circles'. He examined one formation of 36 metres (40 yards) diameter and speculated that it might be the result of a lightning strike.

The events around Warminster in the 1960s and 1970s have been the subject of several books, notably those by Arthur Shuttlewood, a journalist who lived in the town. Things seem to have begun on Christmas Day 1964, with a series of deafening noises, and various strange events continued into 1966. The area became a hotspot for UFO sightings and it was during a 'sky watch' in 1972 that Shuttlewood, apparently, observed the formation of a circle in a grass field. He described a high-pitched hum and a circle being inscribed like 'the opening of a lady's fan'. Circles were again found in this area of Wiltshire during the 1980s.

ESCALATION OF NUMBERS AND INTEREST

In the years following the 1980 newspaper coverage, public interest in the subject grew, and more formalized research groups were established. Total numbers each year remained relatively small and a catalogue of basic types was observed. It seemed that the phenomenon showed 'evolution', with single circles graduating to doubles, triplets and quintuplets, with rings being added, first singly then in pairs. There has never been agreement regarding actual numbers of circles discovered in each year, due in part to differing methods of counting; some databases count 'events' or sites, others count component parts of multiple circle formations. However, overall numbers of circles do seem to have increased through the 1980s, with fewer than 10 sites per year up to 1987, 26 that year, and 50 plus the following year.

Through the 1980s, the circles attracted periodic coverage in national newspapers in the United Kingdom. In 1981 Pat Delgado, a retired engineer, drew the attention of the national media to a set of three circles in the Punchbowl at Cheesefoot Head, Hampshire. In 1983 the *Daily Express* ran a story on the Quintuplet set, again found in the Punchbowl, headlined 'ET phone the Express – have you come back to earth?' This prompted another paper, the *Daily Mirror* to commission a hoax circle, with the apparent intention of discrediting the *Daily Express*. This was exposed by the same investigator, Ian Mryzyglod, who had visited the 1980 circles.

Two events towards the end of the decade had a profound influence on the development of interest in the circles. In 1988 sets of Quintuplets were found in the field adjacent to Silbury Hill, near Avebury in Wiltshire, switching the focus from Hampshire, and beginning a pattern, which has continued since, of circles appearing in profusion around the ancient monuments of the Avebuy area (see cover illustration).

The following year, Colin Andrews and Pat Delgado's *Circular Evidence* was published (see Further Reading). The pair had formed a partnership, an organization called Circles Phenomenon Research, and in collaboration with a small number of other researchers, had visited, recorded and photographed an impressive collection of events, which were detailed in the book. It became a best seller, prompting many people to take an active interest in the circles.

Circular Evidence was not the first book on the subject. Dr Terence Meaden, who had been publishing reports of circles in the specialist *Journal of Meteorology* since 1980, published his own book, The *Circles Effect and its Mysteries* (see Further Reading). This elaborated on his ideas that the circles were a product of atmospheric conditions. In 1987 he set up a research group CERES, named after the Roman Goddess of agriculture.

It was through Dr Meaden's organization that another 1988 event came to light. He reported the experience of Tom Gwinnett, who was driving by his organic wheat field when his car stalled and the lights died. He then observed flashes of light among the wheat heads,

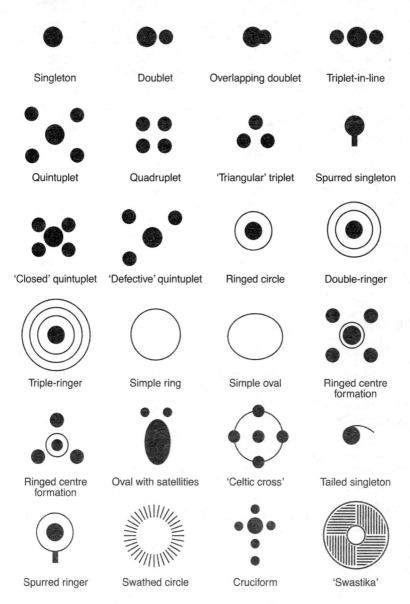

Singleton Doublet Overlapping doublet Triplet-in-line

Quintuplet Quadruplet 'Triangular' triplet Spurred singleton

'Closed' quintuplet 'Defective' quintuplet Ringed circle Double-ringer

Triple-ringer Simple ring Simple oval Ringed centre formation

Ringed centre formation Oval with satellites 'Celtic cross' Tailed singleton

Spurred ringer Swathed circle Cruciform 'Swastika'

The evolution of crop circles

11

converging on an orange yellow light form, which was spinning, emitting a noise likened to an old-fashioned sewing machine. After a minute or so, the light blinked out and his headlights came on. The following day an 8 metre (26 feet) circle was discovered at the site where the light form had been observed.

By the time *Circular Evidence* was published, distinct positions were starting to emerge when it came to considering explanations for what was making the circles. To begin with, researchers had tended to collaborate, but as division crept in, relationships became less cordial. Broadly speaking, the division was between those who sought a natural explanation for events, and those who saw more exotic energies at work. Chapter 4 looks at theories in detail and how they have developed as the phenomenon has.

We have looked at the early days of interest in the circles and seen that there is good evidence that circles have been occurring for many years. The events of the next three years, 1989–91, are remarkable and deserve a chapter to themselves.

REFERENCES

A full bibliography can be found in Further Reading and Resources.

Circles in France and Australia are cited in numerous places, such as Dr Meaden's chapter in *Crop Circle Enigma*. Ian Mryzyglod's investigations are described in Schnabel's *Round in Circles*. Dr Meaden's eye witnesses are quoted at length in his *Circles From The Sky*. Andrews and Delgado describe Simon Brown's references to circles from earlier years in *Circular Evidence*. Bob Rickard's article on folklore in *Crop Circle Enigma* contains information on the Mowing Devil. The events at Warminster are the subject of several books by Arthur Shuttlewood, such as *The Warminster Mystery* and also articles in *The Cerealogist No. 3*. Tom Gwinnet's observation is in Dr Meaden's *Circles From The Sky*.

PRACTICE

LocAL ReseARch

If you live in a rural area, your local library could contain accounts of circles events, hidden away in old records and archives. Old newspapers and accounts of local folklore may be useful.

Try talking to farmers/farming families/farm hands – they may have recollections similar to the ones described in this chapter. If you live in an urban area, try making research trips to cereal growing areas. See Chapter 5 for further suggestions about fieldwork during the circles season.

3 THE GOLDEN AGE
1989–91

SURVEILLANCE ATTEMPTS

1989 saw a large jump in numbers of circles; Dr Meaden's database showing 305 circles that year. It was also the first year that a systematic attempt to 'catch' a circle forming was made.

Andrews and Delgado set up 'Operation White Crow', at the Cheesefoot Head site in Hampshire, with the intention of mounting a 24-hour watch on a known circles location, using infra-red and image intensifier cameras to supplement human observers. For 10 days a team of up to 50 people manned the site in shifts, but no circles formed in the field under surveillance.

The operation did, however, produce two events of note, one of which has passed into circles legend. The first occurred on the night of 12/13 June, when observers saw and captured on videotape an orange stationary light above the field. No conclusive interpretation was made of this.

The second was during the early hours of 18 June, when six participants in the operation were sitting in a circle which had formed some three weeks earlier, with the intention of trying to establish contact with the 'circlemakers'. A strange trilling noise was heard, continuing for some time and appearing to move around, as if under intelligent direction.

One of the participants, George Wingfield, addressed a request to the sound; 'please will you make us a circle?'. The following morning, a

new circle was discovered about half a kilometre (a quarter of a mile) away. The sound was also recorded and has been the subject of controversy since. Some saw it as the 'signature' of the circlemakers, others as the song of the Grasshopper Warbler, a small bird known to frequent cornfields and to sing at night. Its song is a remarkable mechanical whirring noise, which in the absence of a direct observation, is hard to associate with a bird.

Design developments

1989 saw several developments in circle design. At Beckhampton, near Avebury, a ringed circle was found of more than 30 metres (100 feet) in diameter, comfortably the largest found at that time. A circle near Winchester had a curving tail and was nicknamed the tadpole. For the first time 'grapeshot' were seen, scattered across fields like shotgun pellet marks.

But the most significant circles were two which showed a unique lay, with the crop swept out from the centre in four sections at right angles to each other. The centre showed a typical swirl. The importance of these events was the non-circular nature of the lay, apparently contradicting ideas that some form of whirlwind was responsible. These were found at Winterbourne Stoke, in Wiltshire.

Again, during 1989, the majority of circles discovered in the United Kingdom were either in Wiltshire or Hampshire, the CERES database showing only 73 out of 305 circles occurring outside this region.

The publication of *Circular Evidence* prompted much greater media coverage and the BBC covered the subject on several occasions. It was during the filming of one of these items that a noise was recorded which the on-site team was unable to account for. It was described as being like an 'electronic sparrow'. As a measure of the worldwide interest in the circles, John Macnish, the producer, says that the BBC made £120,000 from sales of the recording of this noise.

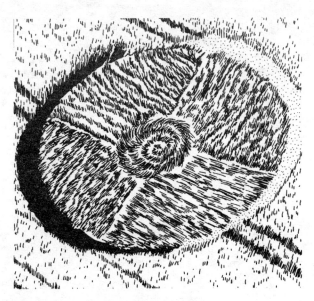

A circle at Winterbourne Stoke, Wiltshire, 1989

1990: The appearance of the pictograms

The 1990 season began with a series of huge circles in the Avebury area, each sporting a delicate outer ring, or rings, including a spectacular triple ringer with four satellites, followed by an even bigger triple ringer, with a circle of 62 metres (203 feet) and an outermost ring measuring 85 metres (280 feet).

If the giant circles in Wiltshire were essentially larger versions of formations seen previously, the next development in Hampshire was a leap into a completely new kind of formation, to which the description pictogram was given. On 23 May the first of these new designs was found, at Chilcomb, consisting of two circles joined by an avenue, with a pair of rectangular boxes on either side. This was followed by a half dozen variations on the same theme, all in Hampshire. The next elaboration was semi-circular rings round one of the circles, rather like a halo.

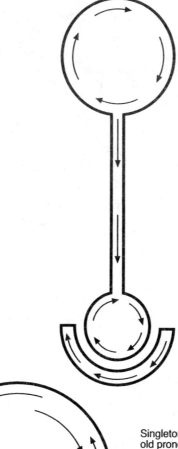

OVERTON HILL
August 2nd '91

Pictogram 145ft

Seven days old*. Some crops growing up again. Well trampled.

Singleton in same field. One week old pronouced banding spiralled clockwise.

Perimeter was thin anticlockwise rim.

75ft diameter.

Two small 'grapeshot' circles in same field.

*Pictogram a month old.

17

Many observers felt that these pictograms proved conclusively that natural forces, such as whirlwinds or vortices, could not be responsible and the arguments over this are covered in Chapter 4.

The eighth pictogram, this time in Wiltshire, became one of the most famous formations to date. Discovered on 12 July, in East field on Tim Carson's farm at Alton Barnes, the formation consisted of two dumb-bell pictograms joined end to end. Added to these were various additional smaller circles and features described as claws or hands, giving an asymetric appearance, the entire formation measuring 119 metres (130 yards). Thousands of visitors flocked to see the pictogram and Carson is said to have made about £5,000 in admission charges. The image of this pictogram was given further life when the rock group Led Zeppelin used it as cover art for a box set of CDs.

Two very similar pictograms followed, one apparently pointing at Silbury Hill, measuring 137 metres (150 yards). Further giant pictograms followed in Hampshire, with a particularly beautiful formation at Hazely Farm, near Cheesefoot Head, which appeared to combine features of both the earlier Hampshire pictograms and the later Wiltshire ones. Outside these two counties, circles were reported from Devon, Sussex, Norfolk, Cambridge, Northants and Lancashire. Circles were also reported in Scotland.

New surveillance attempts

Further attempts to capture a circle forming were made in 1990, with two watches mounted, one in Wiltshire led by Earl Haddington, the other a high-tech affair under Andrews and Delgado's direction in Hampshire.

Operation Blackbird had been planned with John Macnish, the television producer who had recorded the 'Noise' the previous year and involved collaboration with a Japanese television production company. A site was identified at Bratton Castle, on the edge of Salisbury plain, and once again cameras were trained on a field thought to be a probable location of circles. The project was the

Alton Barnes pictrogram

19

subject of coverage by the BBC's *Daytime Live* programme and, on 25 July, Andrews made a sensational announcement to the viewers.

'We do have a major event here ... two major ground markings have appeared in front of all the surveillance equipment.'

Unfortunately, the excitement and optimism that a breakthrough had occurred was short-lived. When Andrews and his partner Delgado entered the formation a few hours later, it was immediately evident that the formation was suspicious. A 'horoscope' board game was found in the centre of each of the circles comprising the rather odd looking formation, and also a length of wire, corresponding to the diameter of some of the circles. It was known that nobody had entered the formation since daybreak and the articles found provided proof, accepted by Andrews, that they had fallen victim to hoaxers.

Andrews later described his premature remarks as 'unfortunate', and, for many people, the episode confirmed that the entire subject was not to be taken seriously. A further circle did form, on 4 August, in the form of a question mark. This was caught on film, but it has never been widely screened, since substantial enhancement was necessary in order to determine anything of significance. It was possible to see that whatever formed the circle had not descended from above, and there were no unexplained lights above the formation.

The Cerealogist

1990 also saw the foundation of *The Cerealogist*, originally edited by John Michell. Starting with the headline 'New wonders in the cornfields', the quarterly journal established itself as a leading publication on the subject, being prepared to print a broad range of opinion and not confining itself to one viewpoint.

Michell had written extensively on Earth Mysteries and ancient cosmology since the 1960s, when his first book, *Flying Saucer Vision*, was published. He maintained a scholarly attitude and tended to focus on the effect the circles had on humans, rather than explanations.

This first edition reported the conference at Oxford, organized by Dr Meaden, which was the first attempt to hold a scientific gathering to address the circles. The conference was addressed by guest speakers from Japan and the United States. Two UFO researchers, Jenny Randles and Paul Fuller also spoke, suggesting that Dr Meaden's ideas about atmospheric phenomena could also explain many UFO sightings.

Colin Andrews challenged Dr Meaden to explain how meteorological theories could explain the case of the giant triple ringer which had 'grown' an extra ring some time after its initial formation. For the physicist, this could only be explicable by hoaxing. The fantastic events of 1990, and those which followed the next year, emphasized the divide between those seeking natural explanations and those who felt that some unknown energy, under intelligent direction, was responsible.

1991

While 1990 had been exceptionally hot in the United Kingdom, the 1991 season began with a miserably wet June. Expectations were high that new developments would occur and, when the season began in earnest, people were not disappointed. The first new symbols were labelled insectograms, because of their resemblance to insect bodies. Found first in Hampshire, they migrated to Wiltshire, with two formations being found near Stonehenge. These designs incorporated ladder-like tails and appeared related to the Hampshire pictograms that had begun in 1990.

Alton Barnes was visited again by the circlemakers, first with a long-shafted pictogram and then a further dumb-bell design. But the undoubted centrepiece of the Wiltshire season was the fantastic geometrical formation below Barbury Castle which appeared on the night of 16/17 July. A double-ringed central circle was surrounded by an equilateral triangle, which had a different circular design attached to each angle; a simple ring, a six-spoked wheel and a ratchet spiral. Each angle was bisected by a line leading back to the centre of the formation.

Barbury Castle, Wiltshire, 1991

The image seemed rich in symbolism, and was variously described as a two-dimensional representation of a tetrahedron, an alchemical symbol, and a demonstration of three in one, the central circle containing the total area of the other three circles.

As the season progressed the area around Avebury became scattered with pictograms. Fine examples of long pictograms in a similar vein to the Alton Barnes formation of the previous year could be seen on Preshute Down and at East Kennet. Double and triple dumb-bells were found at Avebury Trusloe and Hackpen Hill respectively. In late July, a series of 'fish' type pictograms began appearing with the first one near Lockeridge and a second on Firs Farm, Beckhampton.

These formations consisted of a 'body' tapering at each end into a circle and a pair of 'fins' on either side of the body. The centre of the body contained a swirled circle, around which the crop flowed.

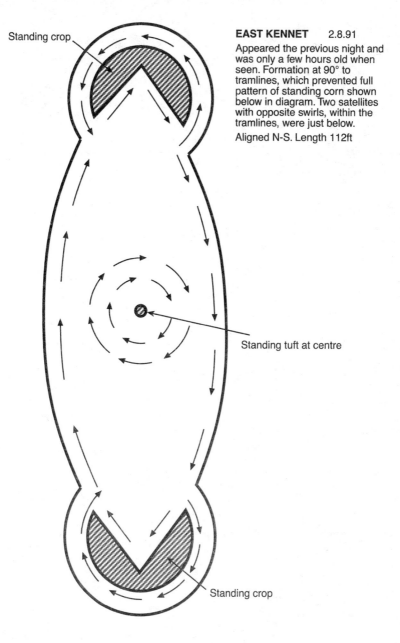

EAST KENNET 2.8.91

Appeared the previous night and was only a few hours old when seen. Formation at 90° to tramlines, which prevented full pattern of standing corn shown below in diagram. Two satellites with opposite swirls, within the tramlines, were just below.

Aligned N-S. Length 112ft

Standing crop

Standing tuft at centre

Standing crop

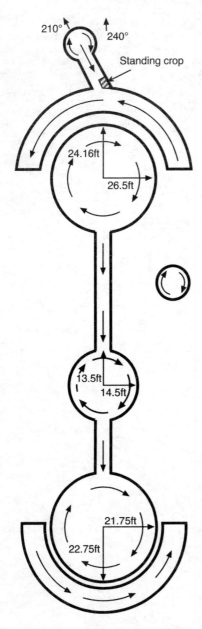

210°

240°

Standing crop

24.16ft

26.5ft

13.5ft

14.5ft

21.75ft

22.75ft

HACKPEN HILL   August 1st '91

Pictogram 246.5ft overall.

Head feature added at a second event, at 30° to main axis. Small outlier added at third event.

24

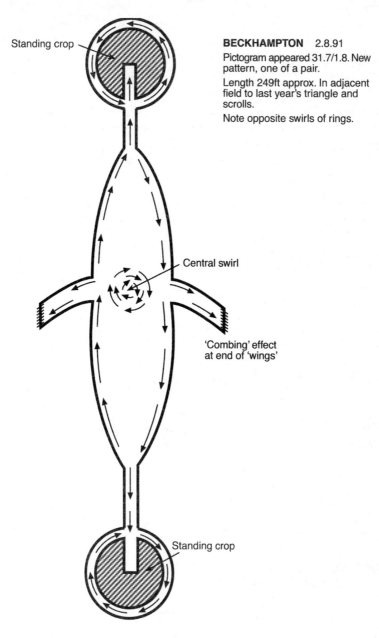

Standing crop

BECKHAMPTON 2.8.91

Pictogram appeared 31.7/1.8. New pattern, one of a pair.

Length 249ft approx. In adjacent field to last year's triangle and scrolls.

Note opposite swirls of rings.

Central swirl

'Combing' effect at end of 'wings'

Standing crop

Several variations on this theme appeared, one of which the author visited early on the morning of its discovery. It is hard to convey the excitement of such an experience. A unique perspective is afforded by the opportunity to examine a circle before it has been trampled by visitors and the detail obliterated.

The season ended with a formation in Cambridgeshire, which was recognized as a representation of the Mandelbrot Set, an image generated in the realm of fractal geometry and named after its discoverer, Benoit Mandelbrot, the Belgian mathematician. Its construction was particularly fine, including lines of single-standing stalks and minute circles.

Mandelbrot formation

The implications of the circles in the 1989–91 seasons seemed unavoidable – there was every indication of intelligent design. The Mandelbrot formation underlined this; whilst the symbolism of the previous designs was open to debate, this was an obvious representation of an image that was well known. The consequences of these developments for the various theories put forward to explain the cause of the circles are discussed in the next chapter.

REFERENCES

The *Operation White Crow* material is drawn from my notes, taken at a talk by Colin Andrews in 1990. The description of the trilling noise also comes from my own notes, from a talk by George Wingfield. Details of the BBC's recording of this (or a similar noise) is described in John Macnish's book, *Crop Circle Apocalypse*. Operation Blackbird is described in the same book and also in Schnabel's *Round in Circles*. (See Further Reading.)

PRACTICE

Much of the significance of the 1990 formations was the obvious implication of intelligent design. Many attempts were made at interpreting the pictograms. Can you detect any hidden pattern? Try constructing the basic shapes, look for the repeated motifs that a codebreaker or cryptologist would use. Is there any sense of logic or evolution? Try using your intuitive faculty on the designs that appeal to you; what do they communicate or inspire? What correspondences to other symbols can you see?

Further reference to interpretations of pictogram meaning are found in:

The Cerealogist No. 12 where Koch and Kyborg write of their attempts to decode the pictograms and communicate with the circlemakers.

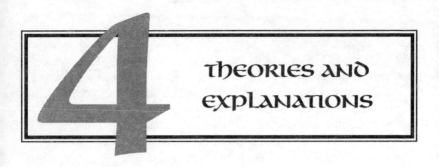

THEORIES AND EXPLANATIONS

This chapter looks at the various ideas that have been put forward to explain the origin of the circles, and breaks down into four areas:

1 Nature traditions and their associated ideas in other cultures
2 Meteorological theories
3 Supernatural explanations, such as UFOs, earth energies and spiritual agencies
4 Hoax explanations.

NATURE TRADITIONS

There is a long tradition of faeries, 'little people' and figures such as Robin Goodfellow or Puck and Jack in the Green, who play mischievous pranks on unsuspecting humans and who have domain over nature. Their importance to pre-Christian societies is seen in the custom of leaving offerings at harvest time. Their existence was taken for granted in a way not easily grasped by the more rational mind-set that prevails today. Even in the Christian era, rural folk would have had little difficulty in ascribing markings in the fields to these type of agencies.

There are some specific associations between faeries and circular markings. Round patches, known to be caused by fungus which increases nitrogen production, resulting in a darker colouring in grass, are known colloquially as 'fairy rings'. Danger attends anyone witnessing faeries dancing in a ring, where humans become enchanted, and dance to their death. Christine Rhone, writing in *The Cerealogist*, quotes John Aubrey, a seventeenth-century antiquarian, from his *Natural History of Wiltshire*, describing the story of a curate who came upon a dancing ring of little people and fell paralyzed. He was attacked with pinches and awoke at dawn inside a fairy ring.

Puck and faery dancers

Robin Goodfellow or Puck is a mischievous sprite known for his tricks on humans and nocturnal revels in the countryside, where flattened grass circles mark the dances of him and his followers. Some observers see these mischievous characteristics in the behaviour of the circlemakers; night time activity and the confusion of human researchers through trickery.

In the east, whirlwinds are personified as djinns or giinis, due in part to the apparent inquisitiveness or mischievousness of their behaviour. William Corliss, in his *Handbook of Unusual Natural Phenomenon*, describes several instances of small whirlwinds displaying what is anthropomorphically seen as curiosity:

I turned and observed a large revolving ring of sand, less than a foot high approaching me slowly. It stopped a few feet away and the ring containing sand and small pieces of vegetable debris in a sheet less than one inch thick, revolving rapidly around a circle of about 12 feet diameter while the axis remained stationary. It then moved slowly around me ... and slowly died down.

Other accounts show very localized effects, such as a fatality that happened in Bradford in 1911, when a narrow funnel-shaped whirlwind picked up and dropped a girl from 6 metres (20 feet), leaving nearby bystanders unaffected.

Meteorological Theories

As described in Chapter 1, a meteorologist was among the first investigators to examine the 1980 circle at Westbury. Dr Terence Meaden had a long-standing interest in tornadoes and other unusual atmospheric phenomena, such as ball lightning. He had founded an academic journal, *The Journal of Meteorology*, which was one of the first publications to include regular articles on the subject of the circles, and also founded an organization, the tornado and storm research organization, TORRO, to research tornadoes and other unusual weather events.

The original case had been referred to him by Ian Mryzyglod, who had heard of his organization through the UFO community, when Meaden had offered an opinion on a supposed UFO sighting.

Meaden checked the weather records for the period at which the circle was known to have arrived, and discovered that the prevailing conditions had been hot and windless. The markings described to him (the field had been harvested by the time he saw it) did not sound like tornado damage, but could be understood as the product of some kind of whirlwind or 'land devil'. These are a species of vortex, caused by thermals, rising air masses.

He began to develop an idea that thermals rising from ground level might be set into a rotary motion by wind currents in the lee of low hills – the surrounding topography at Bratton. He wrote a report for

The Journal and followed this with a further article in 1981, when circles appeared at Cheesefoot Head, slightly refining his first ideas to account for these circles having been found to windward of the hill.

The discovery of the quintuplet sets in 1983 led to the next refinement of the theory. Meaden knew from the literature on tornadoes that the main funnel could be surrounded by smaller 'satellite' tubes and he proposed that the quintuplets could be caused by a vortex with 'minor' vortices held in orbit by a 'standing wave'. This allowed him to predict that systems with three, four and six-fold symmetry might be found as well as circles with arcs.

Critics of his ideas had been quick to point out that, while the idea of vortices could be understood easily enough by reference to the effects visible around buildings when leaves and litter are seen spiralling, the motion of such events is upwards. Whatever was responsible for the circles was obviously a downward force. Meaden developed his idea to incorporate the idea of 'vortex breakdown', a stage in which the rotating air mass assumed an unstable spin, descended rapidly and imprinted the crop.

A further feature of circles reports which any theory needed to take account of was the association of the circles with reports of light phenomena, and the final refinement to Meaden's ideas was a mechanism which could explain these eye-witness accounts. Again, it was known from observations of 'dust devils', that electrical fields can be generated in such structures and that they can emit sound and light. In such circumstances, the air may become electrically charged, or ionized. Such an ionized gas is known as a plasma.

Meaden's idea now looked like this; a rising column of warm air could be given a rotation by air currents, typically in the lee of a hill and, as it rotated, gather an electrical charge, possibly causing sound and light to be emitted, dependent on the velocities involved. If the rotation became unstable the vortex, which would assume a spherical shape determined by surface tension between the charged air of the vortex and the surrounding stable air mass, could drop and be 'guided' down by electrostatic attraction from the oppositely charged crop below. He coined the term plasma vortex to describe this type of event.

Supernatural explanations

Unlike the meteorological theory, there is no single clear-cut 'supernatural' explanation for the circles. We can consider three main types of explanation under this heading: those associated with UFOs, theories based on 'earth energies' and more spiritually inclined interpretations.

UFOs

One of the earliest accounts that we have of a circular ground trace is the 1966 case from Tully in Australia, referred to in Chapter 2. This event is known through UFO research and provides a clear connection between an anomalous aerial phenomenon and circular ground markings. The Warminster circle in 1972 was also associated with reports of UFOs and, consequently, it was inevitable that when close attention to the circles developed in the 1980s it was not long before UFOs were being advanced as an explanation. It is a short step from deducing that the crop has been flattened from above, and observing the generally circular shape, to assuming that a 'flying saucer' has landed.

The UFO community were enthusiastic reporters of the crop circle scene, with the long running British journal *Flying Saucer Review* regularly printing accounts of the latest circles. Researchers Andrews and Delgado and later George Wingfield were made 'consultants' to the journal. *FSR* has reported other circular markings found in association with UFO reports, such as an event in 1967, when a 'milky white cloud-like disc' was observed 'hovering' and circles were subsequently found in the barley crop beneath.

What evidence is there to suggest that UFOs are in any way involved with the circles?

Apart from the appearance of the circles (e.g. early circles such as singles and quintuplets) a number of sightings of aerial forms, either shortly or immediately before circles appeared have been observed. Dr Meaden cites some examples, one of the best cases being Roy

Lucas' observation of a rotating column, surrounded by a white cloud, in June 1988. A few hours later, singletons were found 320 metres (350 yards) away. Tom Gwinnett's observation, mentioned above, is another example.

Randles and Fuller (1990) describe several other events involving eye-witness accounts of aerial phenomenon, such as a nocturnal sighting in Manston, Kent in 1989. A rotating column of blue-white light was seen, accompanied by a humming sound. Inspection of the site where the light was observed revealed two circles in a corn field, one 20 metres (22 yards) in diameter.

Some writers take the association between aerial phenomena and the circles as an article of faith. Alan Watts, in his book *UFO Quest* (see References at the end of this chapter), makes the plain assertion that the circles are caused by intelligently directed UFOs:

> *... I unequivocally attribute the crop designs to UFOs. The answer is that no theory fits the facts other than the designs are being drawn by some form of electromagnetic beam controlled from an invisible UFO.*

In *Circular Evidence*, following a listing of various possible mechanisms responsible for the circles, Delgado acknowledges the possibility of circle producing UFOs, saying:

> *UFOs are claimed to be capable of producing the most extraordinary behaviour and phenomena. Their control of force fields unknown to us may well result in rings or circles. It may well be within the capability of a UFO to manipulate a rotary force field which is enclosed in a sharp cut off electro-magnetic shield.*

A discussion of sub-atomic physics follows, which, it is argued: 'would seem to support the theory that the circles are created by an unknown force field manipulated by an unknown intelligence.'

Palden Jenkins, writing in *The Cerealogist*, in an article entitled 'Communicating with earthlings', says 'I would suggest that the initiative, design and intent behind crop formations originates from ET intelligences... '. He sees the purpose of these as being 'communication with human beings'.

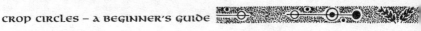
Other writers (Colin Wilson, John Michell and George Wingfield, for example) have drawn attention to the similarities which exist between the UFO experience and the crop circles, in the sense that there appears to be a psychic component to both. This realization arose in ufology as it became clear that many of the elements reported by observers or contactees had more in common with poltergeists, hauntings and other 'paranormal' experiences, than with 'nuts and bolts' flying saucers. These may occur repeatedly to some individuals. UFOs and crop circles share the same characteristic of these episodes of psychic connection occuring to researchers.

Earth energies

The frequent occurrence of circles in proximity to ancient sites such as tumuli, long barrows and hill forts has given rise to theorizing about 'earth energies' as a cause of events. The idea of such energies has a long history but has developed, in recent times, largely from the work of Alfred Watkins whose book, *The Old Straight Track*, described his theory of ley lines. Almost everyone is aware, in some way, of these ideas that ancient sites and natural features, such as hill tops, are connected in straight lines, to which he gave the name 'leys'.

During the 1960s, this concept was elaborated to include the idea that these lines were 'energy lines', and could be detected by dowsing. Many dowsers have suggested that circle formations occur on ley lines and appear due to some sort of build-up of energy. Opinions differ as to whether this is a natural process, or occurs under some kind of intelligent direction.

In outline, the earth energy theories about circles assume that genuine circles will prove to be connected by energy or ley lines to the network of ancient sites. Dowser Richard Andrews describes how they are joined: 'the three line ley is the main reference for the circle configuration, as the circles ... are centrally between these lines'.

Circles would have crossing 'positive lines' at the centre. The actual process of formation is envisaged as a two stage process, with a 'plan' being directed from above, by an unknown intelligence, followed by a surge of earth energy, creating the circle, and establishing a link to the network.

Colin Bloy, another dowser, described the network's energies as: 'subtle, universal, and an aspect of consciousness'.

The 'consciousness' of the energy system might be equated with an 'intelligence' operating from above, to produce the circles. We have already seen that there are observations of UFOs or aerial phenomena in conjunction with the circles, and some writers have speculated that these aerial components may 'seed' a new design, or a new site, following which it becomes active.

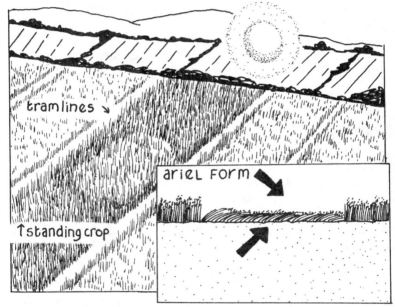

Seeding of circles

The idea that the earth, through its energy system or network, is conscious, forms the basis of the more spiritually inclined explanations. These are, in turn connected to the ecological concerns that have surfaced over the last 40 years. Colin Andrews has spoken on many occasions about his belief that the message of

the circles is one of warning: 'Mother earth is crying'. Allied beliefs include the sense that the earth is receiving energies designed to assist in the raising of consciousness and that circles mark these incoming beams. These ideas are hard to test experimentally.

Finally in this section we touch on a hybrid idea, which draws on several sources. Andrew Collins, in his book *The Circle Makers* (see Further Reading), develops the idea that the circles may be formed through the medium of 'orgone', the name given by Wilhelm Reich to the invisible 'substance' that pervades the atmosphere, given various names in different ages and cultures, such as 'ether'. He sees this as interacting with nodal points on the earth, often the locations of ancient sites, and making crop formations through the emission of ultrasonic waves. The picture is completed by the capacity of orgone to interact with human consciousness. This summary is necessarily brief; Collins' book contains a complex mix of ideas, and is worth reading to understand his ideas in detail.

Ϧoax explanations

Finally, we come to the hoax theory, which proposes that most, if not all circles are the work of human beings. All researchers would accept that man-made events have occurred, the debate is about proportion. Hoaxes have played a part throughout the story, as we have already seen in the case of the operation Blackbird episode, and the tabloid newspapers in the early 1980s.

Advocates of the hoax theory are usually characterized as sceptics. To explain circles satisfactorily as a hoax or man-made event requires two questions to be answered. First, how are they constructed and secondly, why?

Through a variety of sources, plenty is known about the methods employed to construct circles. As well as Doug Bower and Dave Chorley (discussed more fully in Chapter 7), Jim Schnabel has disclosed his techniques and the circle making competition, in 1992, revealed various ingenious strategies.

Early speculation about hoaxing methods included the use of chains or ropes to flatten the crop, but most circlemakers prefer a 'stomping tool' or 'stalk stomper'. This consists of either a plank or length of plastic tubing suspended from a length of rope in a loop, held by both hands, and pushed to the ground in a series of steps, with one foot on the plank. Alternatively or additionally, there are lightweight plastic garden rollers, which may be filled with water for additional weight.

Feet and hands are also used and cardboard or polystyrene sheets employed to spread the load and conceal footprints.

Two basic techniques are used to found a basic circle. Either they are flattened from the centre outwards, which does not necessarily require a stake and line, or using a central point, measured with a length of line, swirled from the perimeter inwards.

Access to the crop is achieved via the tramlines and, by carefully walking through the standing crop, surprisingly little sign of passage is left behind. Often the trademark of a man-made circle is an underlying pathway from the tramline to the centre, which has then been covered over by the swirl of the floor when the main construction is complete.

No doubt the circlemaker's arsenal contains other devices and techniques, but results adequate to have fooled veteran observers have been produced in these ways.

Why people make the circles is considered in detail in Chapter 9, but here is a brief list of possible motives:

- scientific experimentation
- as a 'message' to the 'real' circlemakers
- commercial reasons
- to discredit the phenomenon
- artistic or aesthetic aspirations
- for pure mischief.

A stalk stomper in action

REFERENCES

The material on nature traditions touches on Rickard's article in *Crop Circle Enigma*, and on Brewer's *Dictionary of Phrase and Fable*. Colin Wilson discusses UFOs in his *Alien Dawn* (Virgin 1998). Alan Watts' book is *UFO Quest* (Blandford 1994). Dowsing (referenced more extensively in the resource section) is discussed specifically in relation to the circles in two issues of *The Cerealogist (No. 3* and *No. 4)*, including pieces by Richard Andrews and Colin Bloy.

PRACTICE

How do you evaluate the various theories? If you get the chance to examine a formation at first hand, look carefully at the detail and then consider how the various theories are capable of explaining what you have observed. Can any one theory explain all that is seen? Research reports and records of freak weather in your area, look for reports of circular traces, or luminous balls or discs.

Earth Mysteries researchers have adopted a 'systems' approach, trying to take a holistic approach, encompassing direct experience, scientific investigation, folklore, archaeology and sacred geometry. This is a useful way to investigate the circles; through interconnecting disciplines which can all throw light on the subject.

5

SCIENCE AND
THE CIRCLES

This chapter looks at the various attempts that have been made to conduct scientific investigation of the circles. We have already seen that a scientist, Dr Meaden was amongst the first to take an interest in the subject, but others have tried to apply scientific methods of investigation, with varying degrees of success.

One of the goals of this research has been to find a 'test' which would allow 'real' circles to be distinguished from man-made events, a 'litmus test' for the circles. To this end, much of the scientific work that has been carried out involves testing of samples, either soil or crop, to determine if significant differences can be detected between circle samples and controls from the same field.

Plasma research

We begin by returning to Dr Meaden's ideas about circle formation. These are described in Chapter 4. Here we are concerned with what experimental evidence can show about his theories. As his ideas developed to include the concept that plasmas are involved, he was contacted by Japanese researchers one of whom, Yoshi-Hiko Ohtsuki, had been experimenting with the production of small plasma balls in a laboratory at the University of Waseda.

In 1991 Ohtsuki was contacted by an employee of the Tokyo underground system, who thought he would be interested in a

discovery that had been made by maintenance workers; circular markings left in the dirt on the walls of the tunnels, some of which had rings.

Back in his laboratory, he was able to reproduce a similar effect, through a simple refinement to his existing equipment for generating and observing plasma balls, or 'plasmoids': by placing a tray of aluminum in the microwave chamber, he was able to record the imprint left by the plasmoids. The importance of this was in confirming experimentally that plasma balls could, in a suitable medium, produce rings and circles just as Dr Meaden suggested.

These were very small-scale events, barely comparable with the size of even small circles. However, some of the eye-witness accounts of larger glowing masses in association with subsequent circles, correspond well to what a scaled-up event of this kind could appear like. The unpredictable nature of such events makes detection and recording extremely difficult, as the surveillance attempts described in earlier chapters demonstrate. At Dr Meaden's 1990 conference at Oxford some possible radar evidence of a large plasmoid moving at speed, detected on a ship's radar, was presented.

CROP AND SOIL RESEARCH

The advantage of research directed at samples of crops or soil is in being able to control more of the variables and in being able to apply the results unambiguously to the circle in question.

In 1990 Colin Andrews referred to experiments that demonstrated a 'molecular change' had occurred in samples of grain from a circle. This was later published, as photographs in *The Latest Evidence*, with text asserting that this was proof that any meteorological explanation was 'dead'. Unfortunately, this was to prove as premature as his announcement of a 'major event' at Bratton Castle, since the 'laboratory' in question, in Stroud, Gloucestershire, proved unable to disclose the exact nature of the process used to obtain the 'energy pattern of the crystals' from the sample grain. Subsequent

correspondence from Lord Haddington to the lab operators, on behalf of the Centre for Crop Circle Studies, went unanswered.

Andrews' colleague, Pat Delgado, had sent samples to an American, biophysicist W.C. Levengood, in the same season, and the early reports from his analysis were of more significance. They appeared to demonstrate that plants from within a formation were affected by a rare genetic abnormality, which was absent in control samples from the same field.

The following year a more serious effort, under the direction of Michael Chorost, was undertaken. During the season he collected samples from a number of formations in Wiltshire and, on returning to the United States, subjected these to a variety of tests, on which some fairly sensational claims were based.

Early in the 1991 season, a sample of barley stem from a circle in Cornwall had been examined by a biologist, Kay Larsen. He reported that the nodes of the stem were swollen and the cells appeared to have been subject to an intense heat in a short burst. Chorost's samples, when tested by Dr W.C. Levengood, appeared to confirm this when photographs were produced showing microscopic alterations to the cell walls and a blackening effect where the leaf surface had been been carbonized. Both Levengood and Larsen concluded that the plants could have been subject to a brief but intense burst of energy.

The results came at a time when the hoax theory was widely seen as the most likely explanation. Not only did they appear to show a real, measurable, effect but the control samples, from standing crop in the same field, did not demonstrate abnormalities, neither did a sample from a circle subsequently confirmed as a hoax. It appeared, finally, that some sort of test might emerge, allowing 'real' circles to be distinguished from hoaxes.

Further tests carried out by Marshall Dudley, an independent expert in the design of radiation detection equipment, were also reported by Chorost. Soil samples taken from a number of formations in England, including the Barbury Castle pictogram, were tested. Unexpected results were obtained, with different samples from the

same formation showing both greater and less than average measurements of alpha and beta particles. Another sample from one of the 'fish' formations showed massive readings, compared to a control, of 198 per cent and 48 per cent higher for alpha and beta particles respectively.

Samples from this formation were tested at the internationally renowned Oak Ridge laboratory and showed the presence of 13 radioactive isotopes, most of which had short half lives, indicating that they were not of natural origin. Dudley speculated that these isotopes could have been created by a bombardment of deuterium nuclei.

These results prompted a further project in 1992. *Project Argus*, as it was known, aimed to collect crop and soil samples and subject them to a battery of tests, from seed germination tests to DNA analysis. Volunteers also tested formations for magnetic anomalies, prompted by reports of compasses being affected by residual energies. Magnetometer readings suggested that the soil within several Wiltshire formations had been magnetized and it was theorized that this was caused by the circle-making agency.

Another study, published in 1992, was carried out by Robert Irving and Pam Price and based on the idea that, if the hypothesis that circles were created by a burst of microwave radiation was correct, the populations of bacteria on the plants would be affected, either by a reduction in numbers or in mutation. No significant difference was detected between the circle samples and controls.

Levengood published further results, including a paper in the scientific journal *Physiologia Plantaurum*, which showed that sample plants had alterations to their cell structure. 1993 again saw American attempts to find scientific evidence for the circles when Peter Sorrenson, together with veteran circles researcher Busty Taylor, collected samples of crops which showed signs of 'glazing' with a coating later analysed as iron and oxygen. Further tests showed significant differences between the samples and controls in the growth rate of seeds and electrical conductivity of the tissue around the seed head.

This research which was carried out by Levengood and a physicist, John Burke, led to the hypothesis that particles from the annual

perseids meteor shower had been drawn to the Earth by a plasma vortex and converted to a molten state during entry into the Earth's atmosphere.

Two years later an engineer, Jim Lyons, advanced the interesting theory that the circles could be forming where powerful vertical electrostatic fields interact with points of low impedance on the Earth – the intersections on the Earth's proposed energy grid. Such interactions might cause the formation of nitrogen gases in the atmosphere and nitrates in the soil, therefore testing soil from circle formations might reveal these compounds.

With support from the *Agricultural Development and Advisory Service* (ADAS), tests were done to measure nitrate levels inside and outside formations. The results of these tests showed some suggestions of anomally but, overall, provided no conclusive evidence to support the theory.

Testing human capabilities

Two prominent scientific figures, Lord Zuckerman (formerly the British government's chief scientific adviser) and Rupert Sheldrake, a biologist famous for his concept of 'morphic resonance', had (independently) suggested that the truly scientific approach to the question of whether or not human beings were capable of making circles was to determine experimentally exactly what humans could accomplish.

At Sheldrake's prompting *The Cerealogist*, with sponsorship from the UK newspaper the *Guardian* and the German magazine *PM*, organized a circle-making competition on Edward Dashwood's land in Buckinghamshire in the summer of 1992. The rules of the competition required competitors to work at night, while scrutineers monitored for noises or lights, deducting marks accordingly. The rationale being that, if humans were responsible, they had to be capable of constructing complex formations in the dark, whilst escaping detection, since circles are often discovered in the morning.

The rules also specified precisely the formation that was required and the detailed elements that should be included. The basic design was a dumb-bell, with a circle at one end, and a ring at the other. Various other components, such as grapeshot, an arc, straight boxes and a triangle were incorporated.

Twelve teams entered, and their efforts were judged at daybreak by a panel of judges. The results surprised most people, including the judges and organizers. Jim Schnabel, working alone, had managed to finish second and, but for one mistake, would have won. There was general agreement that the formations would have been capable of taking in most observers, had they been discovered 'unaware', and it was clear that the extent of human ingenuity had been largely underestimated. Several observers commented on the apparently intoxicating effect of producing the circles at night, judged by the reactions of the teams as they came in from the field.

The competition was won by Adrian Dexter's team and, the following day, they gave a demonstration of their technique. Since the formation had to sit between the tramlines, and marks were deducted for signs of entry, they had taken no chances by using an elaborate system of folding ladders to bridge over standing crop and avoided a single central stake hole by using a tripod arrangement as an anchor point for the radius rope.

Evaluating the research

Frustratingly, most of the research described above has not proved to be repeatable (one of the requirements of any true scientific experiment), or later challenged on the grounds of accuracy.

Two main criticisms of Levengood's work were made: firstly the minute differences in the structure which he claimed to have identified required accurate measurement on a scale so small that the magnification used could not allow it. Secondly, the control samples in all these experiments were taken from the standing crop in the same field. It was argued that this did not constitute a true control, since it did not allow the possible effects of 'mechanical' trampling to be considered.

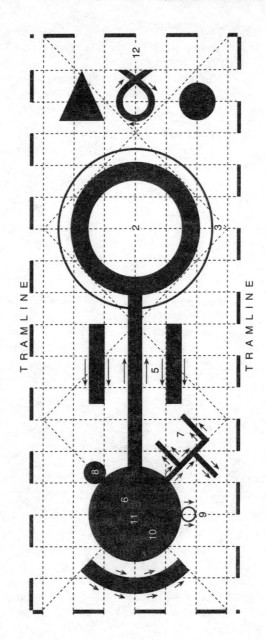

Circle-making competition design

If an unknown intelligence was being proposed as the cause of the circles, the effect of mechanical trampling needed to be excluded as a possible source of the effects being described. Furthermore, to be completely accurate in applying the scientific method, if a flattened control crop was used, it should be flattened at the same time as the circle under investigation.

The samples taken by Taylor and Sorrenson were later claimed to have come from a formation that had been made by Schnabel and others. Rob Irving challenged Levengood to allow an independent test to be carried out to test his assertion that the effect had been produced by a sprinkling of fine iron filings which had been spread over the formation by its constructors. Levengood did not respond directly, but with John Burke and Nancy Talbott wrote to the *Journal of Scientific Exploration* defending their findings. They asserted that 118 of the 130 formations they had tested showed unexpected findings, including increased germination rates and growth from the seeds.

These results were not repeated, which logic dictated they should be, since the earth passes through the perseids shower annually. The radiation results obtained by Marshall Dudley later turned out to be an artefact of the testing system and the procedure used in the lab and the results were not repeated the following year. Thus the 'litmus' test to determine a true circle has remained elusive.

REFERENCES

Main reference for the Japanese scientists' work is Schnabel *Round In Circles*, also Randles and Fuller's *Crop Circles, A Mystery Solved*, and *Circles From The Sky*, by Dr Meaden. The complications of various scientific testing programmes are referenced in Montague Keen's chapter in Devereux and Brooksmith's *50 Years of Ufology* and in the small volume edited by him, *1991 Scientific Evidence for the Crop Circle Phenomenon*. Irving and Price wrote up their work in the newsletter of the Beckhampton Group and in *The Cerealogist*. The circle-making competition is described from my notes of the 1992 'Cornference' at Salisbury. The critique of the research references Montague Keen's contribution to Devereux and Brooksmith's book. (See also Further Reading.)

PRACTICE

OBSERVATIONS THAT CAN BE MADE IN A CIRCLE

The basic design and dimensions should be established; the diameters, lengths and orientation. Record the floor pattern and the lay. Your stride can be used to give reasonably accurate measurements if you do not require absolute accuracy or have a tape measure with you. (Try measuring your stride by marking, with chalk, on a path the position of your feet in a normal stride. Double this then, in the field count double paces, e.g. every time your right foot touches.)

Note the crop type and stage of ripening and date of formation, if known. Photography is obviously useful to record events, so take a camera.

Record the location; the Ordnance Survey grid system is a standard tool for this in the United Kingdom.

THE NEW AGE, THE PARANORMAL AND THE CIRCLES

The circles have had a continuing association with a range of beliefs, ideas and theories that could be considered under the general heading of 'New Age'. They have attracted interest from channellers, visionaries and dowsers. This chapter explores some of these themes and looks at some of the paranormal events that have been reported from within the circles.

Early researchers were quick to notice the proximity of many circles to the numerous ancient sites in southern Britain and, as we have seen in Chapter 4, it has become accepted amongst some researchers that these sites can be connected to the circles by temporary modifications to the local ley system. The primary method used to detect these lines has been dowsing. Dowsing has assumed such importance in investigation of the circles that it is worth considering in some detail.

DOWSING

Historically, dowsing was used to detect underground water and, traditionally, payment for a dowser's services was made by results. This pragmatic approach is important, because it underlines a reality to dowsing, which some of the more extravagant claims made for the technique stretch considerably.

Dowsers generally use a small Y-shaped hazel branch, angle rods or a pendulum. Whilst there is no concrete evidence of how dowsing actually works, there is some consensus that the instrument used,

whatever it is, acts to amplify small muscular movements of the arms, wrists and hands. Some dowsers even claim to be able to dowse with 'bare hands' (Pat Delgado found he was able to dowse in this way).

When dowsing with a hazel 'wand' or rods, the dowser looks for a movement from a stationary 'neutral' position as they walk over or into a hidden line of force, or an underground water course. With a pendulum, a neutral swing is set up and, as either a mental question is asked, or a line crossed, the swing changes to a circular motion, the direction being interpreted as a positive or negative answer.

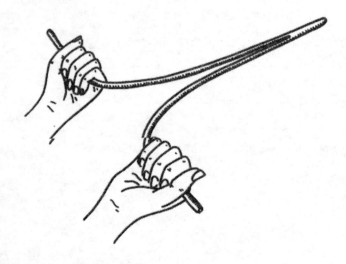

A traditional dowsing rod

Circle investigators who have adopted this method are not confined to the New Age 'true believers'. Dr Meaden, whilst wishing as a scientist to understand dowsing as a response to the ambient magnetic field, used it as a diagnostic tool.

It is said that similar patterns are detectable at crop circles as those found in stone circles, and these findings have led to speculation that the stone circles might mark the sites where 'crop' circles appeared in antiquity. This theme is elaborated in Dr Meaden's book *The Goddess of the Stones* (see Further Reading).

New Age ideology

Amongst the New Age fraternity this connection between ancient sites and crop circles has become an article of faith and is woven in a loose association with ecological concerns, spiritual/earth energies, channelled messages and extra-terrestrial contact. As the early messages of UFO contactees tended to comprise warnings about human behaviour, in the wake of the nuclear age, so the interpretation of the circles' significance has tended to be apocalyptic warnings about our treatment of the Earth. Often these are linked to native American traditions which speak of the Earth as a living entity. Another aspect of this is the belief that human consciousness is undergoing a transformation or shift as we move towards the next millennium.

The case of Mary Freeman's sighting illustrates how these themes come together. Paul Devereux has described how the monuments of the Avebury area can be interpreted as a 'mythic landscape' and Michael Dames' books paint a picture of an ancient worship cycle set round the same sites. This was the backdrop for Mary Freeman's sighting.

On the night of 18 July 1988, she was returning home to Marlborough from Winterbourne Monkton, driving along the stone avenue which leaves Avebury to the southeast. Her attention was drawn to a light in the west. She saw an illuminated column or tube, of a white colour, stretching between the cloudbase and the ground at a slight angle, striking the ground in the vicinity of Silbury Hill. The tube had appeared from a glowing patch on the cloud.

Schnabel's account of this in *Round in Circles* (see Further Reading) describes Mary Freeman experiencing a surge of energy inside her

car as she witnessed this and she later told investigators that she felt 'privileged' to have witnessed the 'ethereal' beam.

Two days later the quintuplet set of circles were found in a field adjacent to the A4 main road opposite Silbury Hill. As described in Chapter 2, these circles, with other sets which appeared subsequently, seemed to provide the whole phenomena with a geographical focus in the 'spiritual landscape' of the Avebury region.

Channelling and paranormal events

A local medium, Isabelle Kingston described a sense of being made aware that the area around Avebury would manifest a sign, two years before the Quintuplets appeared. She may be seen as epitomizing the New Age themes described above, with interests encompassing dowsing, channelling (essentially a new term for the art of mediumship), a belief in the energy system of the Earth and its connection to ancient sites and a deep sense of belonging to the Avebury area.

She later predicted both the location and most of the design of the famous Alton Barnes pictogram in 1990, by using as combination of channelling, which she described as 'thoughts appearing in her head' and map dowsing. This method uses a pendulum, held in one hand while the other points at locations on a map. The responses of the pendulum are observed, while a question is held in the mind.

She also reported electrical malfunctions plaguing her house when engaged in talks about the circles, a regularly reported event by many circles researchers. Colin Andrews describes a succession of similar events which occurred when he had taken a soil sample from a circle into his research office and found his intruder alarms repeatedly triggered, for no apparent reason, over the next few days, with these events clustering at 04:15. This experience probably influenced Andrews' perceptions of the phenomena, for *Circular Evidence* reads as a compendium of other strange effects which took place in or around the circles.

He talks of his experience at Kimpton in 1987, when investigating a ring that had been discovered by Busty Taylor when he was landing at a nearby airfield. After experiencing a 'black flash', which momentarily blotted out the sun, he returned to the site and asked God to give him a clue as to how the circles were created. He then heard a crackling noise reminiscent of static electricity, which reached a crescendo, driving him out of the field.

Almost all circles researchers have had some paranormal experience during their investigations. There have been descriptions of:

- 'black flashes', also blue ones
- photographic anomalies such as the appearance of objects on film not seen when the exposure was taken
- malfunctioning electrical equipment, such as camera mechanisms, tape recorders and video equipment, notably during a BBC filming session
- compasses spinning when placed inside circles
- humans and animals experiencing sickness and discomfort inside circles
- dogs and other animals being disturbed at night when circles are found the following day
- a strange trilling noise, difficult to localize
- episodes of 'lost time'
- healing experiences
- subsequent 'out of body experiences'
- synchronicities, such as researchers dreaming of particular formations, prior to their appearance.

This list is not comprehensive and any researcher you speak to will tell you of their own strange experiences with the circles. These kind of happenings are both an attraction and what makes the circles so difficult. To those who have an interest in the 'paranormal' these events are 'digestible'. To the sceptic, they taint the subject, making it impossible to treat seriously. Indeed, even within cerealogy, the enthusiasms of some of the 'wilder' exponents are something of an embarrassment, a situation familiar to serious ufologists.

Spiritual ideas

Jurgen Kronig, a German journalist who was living in the Beckhampton area in the early 1990s writing in *The Cerealogist*, developed the idea that people's response to the circles are indicative of an emerging world view which is shaped by a rejection of the destructive scientific exploitation of the world. He quotes the young student he met in Avebury, who told him that the circles showed 'where we should build new stone circles to heal the earth'. He goes on to say:

The new world view or religion embraces not only the belief in UFOs and extraterrestrials; it accepts the existence of other dimensions, of non-physical entities in other realities – devas, fairies, spirits, ghosts; it includes the belief in reincarnation and understands our planet, if not the whole cosmos as a living entity.

Stanley Messenger, an anthroposophist, describes a whole history connecting the ancient sites, the emergence of consciousness in humans and the present-day appearance of the circles. These, he believes, are the same images as our ancestors witnessed as manifestations of non-physical beings who guided our development. He interprets the meaning of these events as a warning about our farming methods, the dangers of over-cultivation of one of our food staples and degradation of the soil. Here we see the same essential idea expressed in Colin Andrews' warnings that 'Mother Earth is crying'.

Besides Andrews' views, another founder of a circles research group also talks of a clear spiritual purpose in the circles. Michael Green, who was the co-founder of the Centre for Crop Circle Studies, has always advocated a spiritual origin for the circles, seeing them as a part of an unfolding mystery, showing us a window into other realities. He believes that because of this essential spiritual dimension, which threatens orthodox views, there will never be widespread acceptance of the circles.

REFERENCES

Flashes occurring are reported in *Circular Evidence* and on the *Circlemakers* website. *Circular Evidence* also reports instances of

photographic anomalies and cases such as the one in *The Circular 23* turn up regularly. This photo, part of a panorama of a formation at Roundway Hill, was enlarged to show a discoid shape on the horizon. Macnish in *Crop Circle Apocalypse* details examples of malfunctioning equipment. Lucy Pringle of the CCCS conducted a long-running data collection exercise on physical effects. The episode of the 'trilling noise' is described in *The Cerealogist No.1* by Lord Haddington and, humorously, in Schnabel's book. There are many anecdotal accounts of healing experiences associated with the circles and Pringle's collection of physical effects included both beneficial and harmful effects.

Dowsing references are given in greater detail in the resource section. Specific to dowsing in the circles are articles in *The Cerealogist Nos 3 and 4*, and a small book, *Dowsing the Crop Circles*, from Gothic Image. Dr Meaden mentions it in his first book, *The Circles Effect and its Mysteries*. (See also Further Reading.)

Isobel Kingston's story is told in *The Cerealogist No. 4* and in Schnabel's book. The references to Icke, Messenger and Green all come from my own notes of various lectures.

PRACTICE

Try pendulum dowsing as described in this chapter. A small amount of practice will allow you to become familiar with your own dowsing reactions, and you can use this method to 'answer' questions. This can then be applied to crop circle research. An obvious experiment is to obtain a sample ear of corn from a circle, together with a control from elsewhere in the field. With a friend, you can conduct a blind trial, testing the accuracy of your reactions in determining the circle sample from the control.

If you visit a circle, what are your subjective experiences? Try meditating or contemplation, and note your responses. Approaching these aspects of the circles by direct experience, experimentation and observation will help to evaluate their importance for you as methods of investigation.

When in the field, monitor any equipment you take with you, such as cameras, watches, compasses etc. Do they malfunction?

7

hoax! the circlemakers

Early hoaxes

Randles and Fuller published one of the earliest references to hoax as an explanation of the circles, in their BUFORA booklet, *Mystery of the Circles*. In 1990 they elaborated on this in *Crop Circles, a mystery solved*, which has a chapter on hoaxing, acknowledging that 'it would be foolish for any circles researcher to claim that hoaxing cannot be a realistic answer for at least some of the circles that are appearing.'

They describe being contacted in 1986 by a 'freelance journalist', who claimed to have evidence that he was behind all the circles in the United Kingdom of the last few years. A demonstration was arranged, at which he was accompanied by two others. A circle was produced, using a pole and chain. They circlemakers added the detail that they carried a trowel to fill the hole left by the pole at the centre of the circle. Following the demonstration the journalist commented that: 'It seems to me that everyone has overlooked the possibility that these are a hoax, and that somewhere someone is sitting back killing himself laughing at all the publicity'.

Randles and Fuller commented, with some foresight, that this episode emphasizes the 'need for caution when thinking about the possibilities of a large-scale successful hoax'. It was largely their experience of hoaxing in the UFO scene which had suggested caution in their dealings with the circles: there have been many hoaxes perpetrated on gullible UFO researchers.

Andrews and Delgado discuss hoaxing in *Circular Evidence*: 'It is perfectly natural to ask if the circles are hoaxes, but very difficult to

explain why they cannot be hoaxed satisfactorily.' They go on to describe various attempts to simulate the flattening effect found in the 'real circles'. They concluded that it is impossible to artificially flatten crop without leaving tell-tale traces, such as damage to the plants and footprints and that there are 'certain aspects of true circles that could never be produced ... manually'. Their assertions are important because, appearing in a best-selling book and coming from two of the leading researchers, they became accepted as facts.

Many other researchers made similar statements concerning the difficulty or impossibility of reproducing effects seen in the circles manually or mechanically and the ways in which genuine circles can be distinguished from hoaxes. There had been a number of well-known hoaxes – in particular the 1983 attempt by the *Daily Express* to fool their rival newspaper, the *Daily Mirror*, and the hoax at Bratton during Operation Blackbird – but, up until 1991, there was a large measure of agreement that, while hoaxing occurred, 'experts' were capable of distinguishing between man-made circles and the 'real thing'.

Development of hoax theory

In 1991, however, there were various developments that were to eventually cause a substantial revision of the assumptions described above. Articles in *The Cerealogist* by Peter Williams and Ken Brown drew attention to the existence of a number of issues which were highly suggestive of human involvement in the circles.

Williams was a veteran 'sky watcher' during the UFO flap that surrounded Warminster. Like Randles and Fuller, it was his experience of the activities of hoaxers in this context that made him inclined to scepticism about the origin of the crop circles. He made the point that as well as 'hoaxing' lights in the sky, attempts had also been made to fake 'landing sites' by flattening grasses in fields near Cradle Hill outside Warminster. He suggested that it would be a 'short step' from this to making crop circles as we now see them.

He drew attention to the fact that, despite the claims made that features of 'genuine' circles were impossible to hoax, evidence

existed that human circlemakers, using fairly basic methods, could indeed produce circles which were accepted as the 'real thing' by investigators. In 1991, both Dr Meaden and Busty Taylor were publicly embarrassed by a group called the Wessex sceptics, who had produced a formation in conjunction with a film company. On camera they both, independently, found evidence of 'genuine' phenomena in the ringed circle made by the sceptics.

Ken Brown's investigations were more practically based than Williams', who relied on logical deduction and interpretation, rather than fieldwork. Examining formations at Cheesefoot Head in 1991, he became preoccupied by the existence of 'underlying pathways', which had previously been noted by other researchers, but never really interpreted. He noted that the underlying paths must have been the first elements of the design to have been laid down.

Brown's interpretation of these pathways was that they indicated the line walked by hoaxers as they established the centre point of the circle and which was then covered by the main swirl as it was laid down in a series of widening circles from the centre outwards. As he was coming to these conclusions, a massive shock lay in wait for circles researchers.

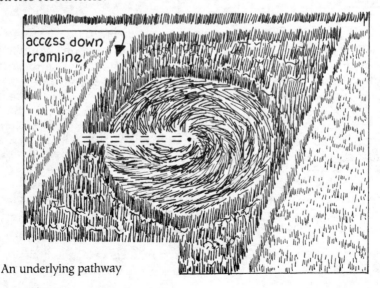

An underlying pathway

Doug and Dave

The day after the Cerealogist 'Cornference' had ended on a high, with participants gathering in the Abbey ruins at Glastonbury to meditate, followers of the phenomenon were brought down to earth by a front page story in the British daily newspaper *Today*. Headlined 'The Men Who Conned The World', the story revealed how two Southampton men in their sixties, Doug Bower and Dave Chorley, were claiming to have started the entire phenomenon, making circles intended to suggest UFO landing marks, after their Friday night sessions in the pub.

The story ran across several pages and included details of a 'sting' that had been perpetrated on Pat Delgado. With the connivance of the paper, the two had made a large pictogram, much in the style of the season's 'insectograms', which *Today* had then informed Delgado about, inviting him to visit it. He had not only authenticated it, but described it as 'the most wonderful moment of my research'.

Later, he was confronted with the news that it had been constructed by Bower and Chorley, witnessed by the reporter, Graham Brough, and the paper's photographer. Brough came to Delgado's house bringing Bower and Chorley with him. They described how, over many years, they had made as many as 20 or 30 circles a year, mainly in Hampshire.

As reported, Delgado's initial reaction was a complete acknowledgement of the claims that Bower and Chorley were making. He subsequently modified this, but the impression conveyed was one of the 'founding fathers' of cerealogy effectively writing off the whole phenomenon. It quickly became the case that Bower and Chorley, despite their actual claims, were being described as responsible for all the circles.

There were many obvious problems with the idea that they could have been responsible for all the circles, not least the circles which had been found outside the United Kingdom, and the eye-witness accounts of circles forming.

When examined more closely their story was fairly specific, both in terms of the total number of circles they had made and the location

of these events. They gave various dates for their first circle, initially reported as 1981, later amended to 1978, and then 1975. They began by using the iron bar from the back door of Chorley's picture framing shop, working on their hands and knees, later devising the 'stalk stomper' described in Chapter 4. Many of their early circles went undiscovered and, when the circles failed to get the publicity that they had anticipated, they began to focus on locations where they could guarantee that someone would see them.

In 1980 they chose a site below the White Horse at Bratton and were rewarded with a report in the *Wiltshire Times*. The following year the Punchbowl site at Cheesefoot Head was planted with crops and they were able to leave circles there. As the subject took off, they maintained some contact with circles' researchers, Bower claiming to have rung Andrews the morning after making circles to tell him of their 'discovery'. They often chose sites that they knew had associations with UFOs, such as Cley Hill near Warminster. The idea that the circles were products of a higher intelligence amused them considerably.

They followed the development of Dr Meaden's ideas, deliberately planning features that they thought would confound him, such as a ring around the circle, or the circles with right-angle lays. In 1990, they designed the pictogram, based on a modernist painting, assuming that the non-circular features would be impossible to reconcile with a meteorological theory.

Their story was challenged on all sides by researchers, some of whom refused to accept any of their claims, believing that they were part of a conspiracy to dicredit the circles. The following year, film producer John Macnish entered into a loose agreement with Doug and Dave, as they became known, whereby they would let him know in advance of their circle-making plans and he would film them, using infra-red cameras.

He spent many hours filming them in action at night and by the end of the 1992 season, had amassed substantial evidence of their abilities, much of which is included in his video *Crop Circle Communiqué II*. They had declined, despite repeated invitations and the £3,000 first prize, to enter the circlemaking competition.

However they were out in the fields, at Aston Rowant, the same night producing their own pictogram. Ironically, this was later shown as an example of the 'real' circlemaker's art, mystically appearing during the competition.

Whilst scientifically sound, the circle-making competition also had some effect in stimulating the English circlemakers and provided an opportunity for notes on technique to be exchanged. There seems little doubt that the hoaxers' capabilities have expanded, spurred on by both competitveness and cooperation. Two Wiltshire farmers to whom I spoke were in no doubt of this; the steady 'improvement' of the designs over the last ten years suggested practice making perfect.

Oṫḥer circlemakers

Back in 1986, Doug and Dave had pressed out the words 'we are not alone' at Cheesefoot Head, which they later said was their response to a second, rival group of circlemakers who they believed were operating in Wiltshire. After 1991, as the implications of their story sank in, increasing efforts were made by researchers to identify hoaxing groups. George Wingfield and Jurgen Kronig wrote several pieces collating gossip, rumour, observation and detective work to name the individuals behind particular formations. Paul Fuller, in *The Crop Watcher*, had been pursuing this line for some time, publishing various details that suggested there were increasing numbers of hoaxers at work all over the United Kingdom, and elsewhere in the world.

Some circlemakers did not even try to hide their identity. Julian Richardson, alias 'Bill Bailey', entered into an agreement with a researcher, Michael Inns, similar to that which Doug and Dave had with Macnish, providing advance information of his plans. In 1993, he made a large, geometrically complex formation in Northants, England, which became known as the 'Bythorn Mandala'. This later became the centre of a controversy which illustrated how difficult it was for some of the circles fraternity to accept the extent of human circle-making.

Through a combination of carefully vague reporting and the fact that nobody in the United Kingdom has yet been prosecuted for circle-making, quite a number of hoaxers have put their 'confessions' on record. As a result of this, a great deal is now known about the techniques and motivations of the hoaxer. At a very conservative estimate there are a dozen teams or individuals who are known to have made circles in England.

Jim Schnabel's book describes his basic techniques; lightweight plastic garden roller, for flattening large areas quickly, and ideal for rings and avenues. The stalk-stomper for producing the spiral effect in the lay. Plain old hands and feet for the smaller details. For some design components a central pole (or accomplice) is used to fix a length of line to define perimeters. While working to a plan, the circlemaker is also open to inspiration, improvisation and error, all depending on the circumstances.

From 1994 onwards, the circles in the United Kingdom began to show new heights of artistry. There was a return to more predominantly circular forms, used in large combinations to make designs described as 'thought bubbles' and scorpions. While deliberately cultivating a certain air of mystery, some circlemakers have become more open about their work.

Two London-based artists, John Lundberg and Rod Dickinson, emerged as leading circlemakers and their controversial activities can be monitored from the Circlemakers website. Among these pages one can read other confessions of circlemakers and find a beginner's guide to circlemaking, detailing the tools and methods necessary to make 'genuine circles'. They and others have undertaken commissions. Lundberg's team were flown to New Zealand to perform for NBC and Adrian Dexter, winner of the circles competition, swirled the *Soil Association* symbol, to promote this organic farming organization (still only 1 per cent of UK agriculture).

Interestingly, the circlemakers themselves often profess a belief in the 'real' phenomenon, and also report some of the same experiences of unexplained lights and sounds as described in Chapter 6. On Lundberg's website, he writes 'our crop forms are intended to function as temporary sacred sites in this (Avebury) landscape', and says that

Scorpion formation

their activity attracts anomalies and is the 'subject of attention of paranormal forces'. The motivation of hoaxers and the interaction of humans and the circles is the subject of the next chapter.

A kind of symbiosis now exists between the hoaxers and the croppies, who sometimes allow a grudging respect for the undoubted artistry of the hoaxers. In turn, the hoaxers depend on the croppies for the 'oxygen of publicity', without which their creations would remain obscure and witnessed only by the combine harvester driver.

REFERENCES

The 'tabloid hoaxes' are revealed in Randles and Fuller. Meaden and Taylor fooled is from my own notes and Schnabel's account. The Doug and Dave story is told best in Macnish, particularly his own association with them. Wingfield and Kronig's articles on hoaxing appear in *The Cerealogist Nos 7–9* and *No. 13*. (See Further Reading for website addresses and a full bibliography.)

PRACTICE

How do you evaluate the claims of Doug and Dave? Try examining pictures of formations and work out in detail how and if they could have been constructed using the techniques described in this chapter. How easy would this be at night? Take into account the circle-making competition.

Brown supplemented his fieldwork with careful inspection of pictures and methods, such as counting the rings that were visible and applying some basic mathematical analysis, to arrive at figures for the plank width and average step length used.

If you get the chance to examine a circle at first hand, look critically at its construction and such features as underlying pathways, post holes and its relationship to the tramlines. Check out the circlemakers' website. This will give you a flavour of the way the circlemaker thinks and operates.

8

PARANOIA AND CONSPIRACY

We began with the point that the history of the crop circles resembles that of UFO research and it may be observed pessimistically that little or nothing has been learned from the latter. We have seen in the preceding chapter that circle-making has its roots in UFO hoaxes and the sensitivity of some researchers to this led them to adopt a more guarded approach to the circles. Others have been less cautious. Like ufology, circles research has become prone to paranoia and conspiracy theory and the themes of this chapter constitute some of the strangest episodes in cerealogy.

GOVERNMENT INVOLVEMENT?

Following the hoax at Bratton Castle, during the highly publicized Operation Blackbird, a story began doing the rounds, to the effect that the hoaxers were a special army unit and the motive behind their deployment was government discomfort at the escalating public interest in a phenomenon which appeared to have no obvious rational explanation.

George Wingfield, in *The Cerealogist*, expounded this idea, suggesting that the key to the affair was in the objects found in the circles, when they were inspected by Andrews and Delgado. These were reported variously as 'ouija boards', zodiac or horoscope games, wooden crosses and a length of line, corresponding to the

diameter of several of the circles in the formation. The crucial question was why, having made a formation under the noses of the surveillance operation, the makers had then left obvious pointers to the fact that this was a man-made event?

Wingfield described receiving information from a friend who had a contact in a 'senior position' in the army, who had 'supplied sensitive information in the past'. The information was nothing short of sensational; the formation had been made by a detachment of troops, on the orders of 'the Government'.

Connecting all this with similarly anonymous reports that the circles had been discussed 'at Cabinet level', Wingfield concluded that the items found in the circles were there precisely in order to identify the circles as hoaxes, in order that, very publicly, the circles phenomenon would be seen as nothing more than a hoax.

There were elements of the hoax which were suggestive of inside knowledge of the surveillance operation. It occurred on the second night of the operation, at a time when neither Andrews nor Delgado were there, at a crucial distance from the observation post, just out of range of the image intensifier equipment. Seemingly, the hoaxers had known of the protocols which required that nobody would enter a formation until Andrews and Delgado were on site and had predicted correctly that an anouncement to the media would be made immediately.

There were also facts which demonstrated a certain amount of military involvement, at least in the surveillance operation. The observation post was owned by the army and two soldiers were in attendance throughout the operation, equipped with night sights. They were said to have been absent on the night that the hoax occurred.

John Macnish says in his book *Crop Circle Apocalypse* that he equipped the soldiers with supplementary gear to conduct their own independent surveillance, following the hoax, and that they later shot some film of an unidentified light. Their position seemed ambiguous: they were said to be off duty, yet dressed in uniform.

DISINFORMATION

From this point on, there was increasing reference to 'disinformation', the practice of government supplying false information to its citizens. When the Doug and Dave story broke, there was much opinion that their activities, if to be believed at all, were explicable in terms of government propaganda, intended to portray the circles as an obvious hoax, thereby defusing a growing belief system. Jurgen Kronig and George Wingfield gave voice to this strand of thought. They both wrote, and spoke to the author, of these ideas in 1991.

Kronig elaborated on the rationale for possible government action, also citing the Cabinet-level discussion that was said to have taken place in September 1990. He compared the crop circle believers with the kind of dissidents that governments have often monitored and conspired against. Prior to the break up of the communist bloc, it was radical or revolutionary left wing groups that attracted this attention. In the 1990s, New Age beliefs could be seen as a subversive element.

Wingfield tried to take apart the mechanics of the newspaper story, starting with the copyright tag 'MBF Services', which had appeared at the end of the story. No news agency of this name could be traced. Checks at Companies House, where details of all British companies are registered, showed a few MBF titles, one of which was a farm not far from Wingfield's own house in Somerset. Suspicion increased when it was discovered that the owner of the house and business did classified scientific research and 'consultancy work' for the government.

Pursuing enquiries as to how the government might propagate disinformation, Wingfield discovered that the creation of a phoney news agency identity was a classic method for feeding material to the press. *Today* was a newspaper with falling circulation (it later folded) and he believed that it had been specifically targeted for this reason, as a paper keen to secure an exclusive.

It was against this background that the 1992 season began, with the consequence that elements of suspicion, occasionally amounting to paranoia percolated through the circles. There was an increased

reluctance for any of the prominent investigators to identify any particular event as genuine, for fear of being 'set up' in the way that Delgado, Meaden and others had been the previous season. It had become abundantly clear that there were indeed, well organized circle-making operations taking place and this situation was given another twist when it emerged that circlemakers had 'infiltrated' various research groups.

The circles group at Beckhampton, near Avebury, disbanded when it became known that a prominent member had 'previous form' as a UFO hoaxer. Rumours abounded as to the identity of various circlemakers and the Schnabel and Macnish books make it clear that some people in the circles scene were leading a 'double life'.

The crop circle world had come to resemble the UFO scene, with accusations and counter accusations flowing and conspiracy theories explaining and incorporating each new development into their frame of reference, much in the manner of the characters in *Foucault's Pendulum*. In this atmosphere, co-operation between researchers became less frequent and relationships between rival theorists deteriorated, often to the level of petty insinuations and gossip.

Some researchers found their projects being deliberately targeted by hoaxers. The Argus project were the victims of this, as was Steven Greer, an American ufologist, who claimed success at initiating contact with 'alien' UFOs. He came to Wiltshire in the United Kingdom in 1992, to undertake a project, using high powered lights, which he had used to 'vector in' UFOs in previous attempts. On this occasion, it appears that the sense of expectancy created in his group allowed a group of hoaxers to fool them with some lights shone from a hill some distance away. Understandably, researchers felt hugely frustrated by these kind of events, leading to a situation where writers such as Wingfield were vilified for being 'negative' when they tried to deal with the extent to which mischief makers had become inextricably linked with the circles.

John Macnish describes an episode in his book *Crop Circle Apocalypse*, which illustrates just how strange some of the fringe

areas of circles research are. After being contacted from Australia by a television producer, who was interested in following up the Doug and Dave conspiracy theory, a request for film footage of the farm where MBF consultancy was based was received and included the request that Macnish destroy the letter. Footage was duly shot by Macnish, who then received a late night telephone call from Australia. His caller was the television producer, begging for help, saying he had been holed up in his flat, convinced that he was being spied on by his neighbours and that this was connected to the crop circles.

A further telephone call from one of the producer's colleagues produced the explanation that he had been diagnosed as suffering from a psychotic illness. This prompted Macnish to wonder about 'the real effect that the circles were having on people. I was becoming convinced that involvement with them could have serious side effects.'

Patrick Harpur's article, 'Delusion, revelation and reality', in *The Cerealogist* is a brilliant analysis of the dangers of obsession with the circles and how there is a thin line between the awestruck attitudes of researchers and the development of delusional ideas concerning 'the truth' and conspiracies against the circles. One can observe a current example in the treatment on the Internet of the NBC television programme featuring circlemakers in action.

The next chapter takes a closer look at the psychological aspect of the circles.

REFERENCES

The Bratton Castle hoax is documented in Wingfield's piece in *The Cerealogist No. 2* and is taken from my notes of Colin Andrews in 1990 and various personal communications with other researchers. Macnish gives a good 'inside account'. Kronig's references to Cabinet discussions comes from my own notes of a talk and conversation with him. The story of Henry Azadehdel is told in Keen's contribution to Devereux and Brooksmith's *50 Years of Ufology*. Schnabel's 'CIA links' were referred to in Wingfield's story

on the Alien autopsy scam, in The *Cerealogist No. 15*. The reference to the deterioration of the scene comes from my own observations. The hoax on Steven Greer is described in *The Cropwatcher 15* by Robert Irving.

PRACTICE

Is it possible that the government, the military and intelligence agencies are involved with the circles?

9 PSYCHOLOGY AND THE CIRCLES

This chapter approaches the question of why people are interested in the circles and looks at the effects they have on humans! The connection between the mind and anomalous events is looked at, in the light of Earth Mysteries research, and we explore some of the motivations of human circlemakers.

The appeal of the circles

The most obvious attraction of the circles lies in their aesthetic appeal. This rests on their shape, symmetrical organization and in their colouring and setting. Photographed from the air, the fields show a pleasing contrast between the straight parallel tramlines and the swirled flowing circular designs. The best of the complex shapes show a combination of circular and linear features, which have a harmonious effect on the senses.

Our origins as humans are as hunter gatherers and this deep layer of our psyche has characteristics which reflect the evolutionary pressures of this mode of existence. The capacity to sort, categorize and map were vital components of the natural history intelligence domain, which enabled these early humans to forage effectively. In addition, the capacity to read and interpret signs in the natural world are characteristic mental activities that natural selection has shaped. I believe these origins are reflected in our fascination with collecting; almost everyone possesses some kind of collection, often to the amusement of others.

Part of the attraction that events like crop circles hold can be understood by our response to the stimulus of a sequence of eye-catching artefacts in the natural environment. We are prompted to 'collect' and catalogue these events and then to try and understand their occurrence. The scientific approach to any subject requires a 'stamp collecting' phase, in which data is collected and sorted before it can be analysed or interpreted. This activity has been at the heart of circles researchers' endeavours in the field and in the air, and produces the stream of images that have sustained massive worldwide interest in the subject.

Thus the aesthetic appeal of the circles combines with a strong instinct to observe and categorize events in the natural environment. When these components are added to our appetite for the mysterious, we begin to see how individuals can become obsessive in their involvement with the circles. It is a truism to say that we love a mystery. Actually, we love a mystery when it has what appears as a satisfying explanation, as evidenced in our enduring consumption of 'whodunits'. We would be intensely frustrated by a detective story in which there was no pay off at the end, or explanation of the preceding events.

This desire for solutions has fuelled the attempts of researchers to explain the circles, which can be seen as more indicative of the individuals' psychology than anything objective about the circles themselves. The history of circles research may be seen as one in which insufficient 'stamp collecting' has been done, with individuals imprinting their own particular preconceptions on the data, sometimes shoehorning the facts into their own particular theory. A variety of motives can be seen; the desire for notoriety or celebrity, the need to uphold science or to challenge it, or to bolster a minority world view, even a political agenda.

To the scientist a naturalistic explanation appeals, while the mystic prefers a supernatural one, and our own inclination to either of these standpoints is a measure of individual psychology and not an objective choice. The circles can be seen as a gigantic Rorschach test which allow the viewer to project their own meaning on to the shapes that appear in the fields.

Effects on people

Many people involved with the circles have commented that the subject has had both compulsive and life-changing effects. Jim Schnabel describes his circle-making in this repect: 'knowing helplessly that only the harvesters could free me from this addiction'. Another self-confessed circlemaker, Chris Kenworthy, wrote that 'the danger with hoaxing is that its addictive quality ... can lead you astray'. Equally, those involved in the investigation of circles are affected. George Wingfield described his reaction to the 'Mandelbrot' formation, desperately trying to arouse the same level of interest in others as he had and being incredulous that it was not the main news story of the day. More than one investigator has given up their day job to pursue the circles, Wingfield and Andrews being among the best-known examples.

But what takes individuals beyond the initial aesthetic attraction and has motivated such large-scale interest in the circles? One explanation may be found in the idea of the collective unconscious, itself essentially an ancient idea, which was articulated in Jung's writing. He formulated a model of the psyche in which the personal unconscious of an individual is underlain by the collective unconscious of the entire human race. This may be conceived as a giant storehouse of all human experience, in which the essential elements of all human life exist as archetypes. These may lie dormant, or become active, according to the outer situation in the life of the individual or the world at large. When the outer situation prompts it, the appropriate archetype is activated and images, thoughts and behaviour patterns are released.

The mandala, an ancient symbol, is an example of the way in which an archetypal content may be manifested as an image. It consists, in its simplest form, of a circular design which, according to Jung, represents psychic wholeness and appears in chaotic situations, when there is a need for a focus, to prevent disintegration. At the close of this century the confusion and complexity of human affairs, the apparent inability of government to deal with pollution, famine and the threat of nuclear war, provide the climate in which we might

expect to see mandala symbols. This was Jung's interpretation of reports of flying saucers in the post-war period; circular objects seen in the skies at a time of collective psychic need. He drew historical parallels from previous centuries to show that visionary sightings of aerial objects were nothing new.

Barbury figure construction

The relevance of these ideas to crop formations is in their basic circular shape, which provides the ideal vehicle for the projection of unconscious contents. The appearance of these shapes may affect people at a deep level, because of a collective hunger for signs of order amongst the chaos of the world. Their circular shape corresponds

to a pre-existing 'template' in the psyche and, consequently, just as 'flying saucers' do, the circles are capable of exercising an attraction which can amount to a compulsion. They are events which are neutral in themselves, but which we invest with meaning.

ḣuman–environmental interactions

The process, whereby events occurring in the natural world are interpreted and given significance has an ancient history, stretching back to our origins. Flights of wild birds, the movements of animals, shooting stars and so on have traditionally been understood as ways of predicting the future. The inter-relationship between human consciousness and the natural world has been explored by Paul Devereux, in his book *Earth Lights* (see Further Reading), where he proposes a natural explanation for many UFO sightings, in terms of geophysical processes associated with fault lines.

An example of this occurred in Wales, in 1904–5, when the area around Barmouth became known for sightings of coloured lights, in the form of balls or columns, which were sometimes seen to emerge from the ground. Devereux postulates that these were caused by ionized gases escaping from the major fault line in the area. He used an impressive amount of solid research to support his ideas, citing research by Dr Michael Persinger, a Canadian scientist, who has studied neuroscience, psychology and physiology. He has shown how exposure to magnetic fields and electrical charges can affect human consciousness. Thus humans in the vicinity of earth tremors, fault lines or atmospherically produced field effects may experience percepetual disturbances.

The fascinating aspect of this outbreak of lights, the 'earth lights' of his title, was the close connection between the lights displays and a religious revival that took place at the same time. This was centred around a charismatic individual, Mary Jones. Contemporary

accounts describe how some witnesses of the lights would end up at her chapel seeking spiritual guidance. The lights were incorporated into the prevailing religious beliefs of the day, as a response to the sense of awe that they created. Devereux speculates that these events might demonstrate what happens when a sacred site becomes 'live'.

Fifty years later, the same kind of stimulus – lights seen in the sky – was interpreted in a different way, one which reflected the change in perception of a population who had seen the space race begin. The events at Warminster discussed in Chapter 2 were, this time, seen as flying saucers, or UFOs. A cult grew up around the location of the sightings, just as it had done in Wales earlier in the century. It appears that we have a predisposition to try to fit anomalous events into some kind of framework and this tendency usually expresses itself in what can be broadly termed a spiritual sense.

The response of many to the crop circles as they took hold of public consciousness has been to interpret them as divine or spiritual messages. This has been flavoured by the concerns of the times: growing ecological awareness and the need for some sense of hope or salvation from the problems we face. Mary Freeman's sighting at Avebury and the subsequent circles provided the focus for the development of what can be understood as a cult, complete with its own belief systems, as wary of any attempts to examine sceptically the foundations of these beliefs.

One way of understanding the common core of these three sets of events, Barmouth, Warminster and the circles around Avebury, is through the process by which we project our unconscious needs, desires and fantasies on to strange events in the natural world. These projections always reflect the times; what is known as the *zeitgeist*, or spirit of the age, and the meanings ascribed to the appearance of the circles are an example of this.

Psychology of the circlemakers

Finally in this chapter we turn to the question of the psychology of the human circlemakers. We touched briefly on their motivation in Chapter 4. The more obvious of these explanations have parallels in other cases outside the world of crop circles.

Hoax for financial gain has a long history in the art market and, interestingly, the exact status of a number of works ascribed to great painters, in collections all over the world, is open to debate. In 1983 the *Sunday Times* newspaper was taken in by a forgery of what they had been assured were the genuine diaries of Adolf Hitler, having paid a large sum of money for them. In such cases, where there is a lucrative marketplace, there is a straightforward motive. It is hard to make a direct connection between circle-making and financial gain, unless one believes that farmers who charge entry to circles in their fields would produce or commission such events.

Two further motives, circle-making to 'discredit' supernatural explanations and circle-making as pure mischief making, actually have much in common. Instead of relying on debate and logic, some sceptics have constructed circles, to 'prove' that researchers are unscientific and credulous and that the phenomenon is only the result of human activity. It is the covert nature of their work, and the wish to have their work assessed as genuine, that connects them to the mischief-makers. Doug and Dave are perhaps the most obvious examples of these, although both men painted, and would probably claim some artistic intent. Their satisfaction lay chiefly in fooling others and this is evidenced by reports of their presence among researchers and visitors to circles, observing and questioning people's reactions to their creations.

The motivation of those who produce circles as scientific experiment and those who do so as 'land art' are relatively easily understood, but from the psychological viewpoint, those who engage in circle-making as an act of communication or ritual are more interesting.

In an article entitled 'The Templemakers', Andrew Collins looks at 'paranormal aspects' of human circlemakers' activities, suggesting that the act of swirling a circle can be equated with a ritual magician drawing down a 'cone of power' in a magic circle. From this idea, it is a short step to wondering what effect this may have on the circlemakers, and even to speculating that they may not always be aware of exactly what prompts their behaviour.

Collins says that his enquiries revealed at least one group whose mode of operation he compares to automatic writing, a process during which a trance-like state is entered and the hand holding a pen is directed from beyond the conscious mind to produce messages. These circlemakers see their work as supernaturally directed and every bit the genuine article. Such individuals are deeply caught up in an obsession with the circles. Even mischief-makers like Doug and Dave have spoken of a sense of wonder at what had driven them on to create circles.

Any attempt to understand what is taking place in the continuing occurrence of the circles needs to take account of their effect on humans, both individually and collectively. This aspect of research is as important as fieldwork in the circles themselves.

REFERENCES

The concept of domains of intelligence comes from Steven Mithen's fascinating book, *The Prehistory of the Mind*. Rorschach tests were designed by Hermann Rorschach, a Swiss Psychiatrist, in 1921 and use a series of abstract inkblot pictures to reveal the subject's personality and unconscious motivation. Chris Kenworthy's confessions appeared in *The Cerealogist No. 11*. Wingfield's frustration is revealed in *Harbingers of Change*. A good introduction to Jung's ideas can be found in *Introducing Jung*. His thoughts on 'flying saucers' can be found in his book *Flying Saucers – a Modern Myth of Things Seen in the Sky*. The events at Barmouth are described in Devereux's *Earth Lights* and Collins' article appears in *The Cerealogist No. 8*. (See also Further Reading.)

practice

The study of the psychology of the circles begins with your own interest in them! What interested you in them? Recall your first exposure to them and your reactions. Observe your family and friends' responses to them. What does their reaction tell you about them? What does it tell you about the circles?

Another way in to this process is through the use of 'active imagination'; try drawing or painting mandalas and observe a sequence of them over a period of time. Do you experience these forms as powerful expressions of your own inner life?

The kind of local research described at the end of Chapter 2 could turn up examples of focal points or people around which anomalous events have clustered.

10

the circles
worldwide

While this book has tended to concentrate on events in the United Kingdom, some of the most significant circles events have happened elsewhere in the world. This chapter looks at some of them, starting with a return to the beginning of the story.

Australia

Chapter 1 described the Australian event known as the Tully circles, which were found in 1966, by a banana farmer, George Pedley. Although the case has been reported in countless UFO books since, much new material was uncovered and published in *The Crop Watcher*, showing that this was only part of a much larger catalogue of events. In addition to the 9 metre (30 foot) circle found immediately following the UFO sighting, a further six 'nests' were discovered. The first 'nest' followed a spate of UFO sightings in the area and a local researcher, Claire Noble, has recorded as many as 86 circular markings between 1965 and 1992. The local aboriginal legends recognize the occurrence of lights in the sky, which they attribute to an ancestral spirit known as Chic-ah-Bunnah.

This appears to be one of the longest running cases where aerial lightforms have been observed, circular ground traces have been found and, importantly, it pre-dates by some years the earliest date that has been claimed for man-made circles. All the circles reported from the Tully area have been small simple events and Australia does not seem to have had many occurrences of the kind of large complex shapes familiar in Europe.

Canada

Another country which has a long history, pre-dating the UK outbreak, is Canada. An event in Regina, Saskatchewan in 1974 has parallels with the Tully case. A farmer was working in an oil seed rape field when he saw what he, initially, took to be a hunter's hide. When he approached it appeared to be a revolving hemisphere with the appearance of stainless steel. He observed that the vegetation beneath was moving and turning. As he returned, in a state of some shock, to his tractor he realized that there were four similar objects. He continued to observe them for about 15 minutes until they lifted off vertically, leaving a grey vapour. When he inspected the area over which they had hovered, he discovered that there were ring markings of flattened grass, of about 3.5 metres (11 feet) in diameter, with standing grass in the centre. Circles have continued in Canada, with at least 14 reports in 1998.

Much work has been done on the Canadian circles by Chris Rutkowski, who has compiled an impressive database, with much assistance from Ted Philips' *Physical Trace Catalogue*. This is a massive listing compiled at the end of the 1970s by the Centre for UFO studies, covering both the United States and Canada. Whilst caution dictates that a proportion of these will be UFO hoaxes, there is nevertheless good evidence here for a phenomenon dating back to 1920. Of the 407 cases analysed by Paul Fuller in 1994, more than a third involved flattened circles or rings in vegetation, either natural or cultivated.

United States

In the United States, unambiguous circles (e.g. circles in cultivated crops similar to the UK crop circles) appeared in increasing numbers from 1990 onwards, mainly in Mid West states such as Missouri and Kansas. Whilst a lot of American researchers have directed their attention at UK formations, the phenomenon continues in the United States, with the International Research Centre of Unexplained Phenomenon (IRCUP) listing at least 16 sites in 1998.

A particularly fine pictogram was found at Charlottesville, Virginia of a form not previously seen. It comprised a central circle with three arms, each of which had a small circle at mid length and a larger one at the end. Other pictograms were found in Oregon, including another highly original design, a circle with hieroglyphic-type attatchments.

Japan

The Japanese have been among the first outside the United Kingdom to take an active interest in the circles and researchers have travelled to the United Kingdom to see the circles there at first hand. As described in Chapter 5, they have also been at the forefront of attempts to examine the phenomenon in a scientific manner. Research into plasma balls has produced evidence from two sources, the laboratory and the underground system, to back up the case for the plasma vortex theory for crop circle production. A number of circles have been reported in Japan, mainly in rice crops and of simple forms.

Europe

Circles have been reported from several European countries including the Netherlands, Germany, Sweden, Bulgaria and Hungary. One case from Hungary is notable for involving, what seems to be, a unique prosecution of circlemakers. In 1992 two teenagers made a 36 metre (118 foot) circle which, in due course, was declared to have been made by UFOs and was visited by thousands of people. Subsequently, the teenagers went on national television and produced 'before and after' pictures to prove that they had constructed it. The farm collective then sued them for Fts. 630,000, (roughly £5,000) an amount later reduced substantially in court. The Hungarian Skeptics provided the teenagers with financial support and, the following year, they were awarded the James Randi prize, which he had founded on a visit to the country, for the best scientific investigation of a paranormal phenomenon.

Germany too has had a circles case which caused long-running controversy, beginning with the spectacular set of circles at Grasdorf, in Lower Saxony. This formation was one of 26 found in Germany in 1991 and comprised 13 circles, with cross formations, the whole set measuring 91 by 46 metres (300 by 150 feet). Like many UK circles, it was on a site of archaeological importance and accompanied by reports of unusual lights in the sky. The site attracted many visitors, one of whom located metal objects beneath the ground in three of the half-ringed circles.

The finds were spectacular: three large plates, one of which bore a design identical to the pictogram. The finder disappeared from the scene, later contacting a newspaper and then visiting a jeweller with the editor, where the three plates were identified as being made from gold, silver and bronze respectively. Allegedly, the gold plate was sold and investigations by FGK, a German circles group, threw suspicion on the farmer for having orchestrated the whole affair, although they were inclined to accept the circles themselves as genuine.

A recent estimate puts the number of circles worldwide at 8,000. Even accepting this as a 'guesstimate', it is clear that the circles are an established phenomenon, with no national boundaries, dependent only on a suitable medium to appear in and someone to report their occurrence.

REFERENCES

The Canadian circles are detailed in Randles and Fuller's book and *The Crop Watcher 21*. Information about US circles comes from the Internet. The story of the Hungarian circlemakers is told in *The Crop Watcher 14*. The saga of the Grasdorf pictogram is told in two articles in *The Cerealogist, Nos 12* and *18*.

11 PUTTING IT ALL TOGETHER

This book has aimed to introduce you to the circles and provide you with the starting points for your own investigations. This chapter tries to summarize what we have seen along the way and, with the benefit of hindsight, revisits some of the main ideas about the circles.

We saw at the beginning of the story how the circles have been inextricably linked with UFOs, which might be described as a mixed blessing. On the positive side, this connection has provided circles research with some of its best historical evidence for the existence of the phenomena, since UFO groups have often recorded 'ground traces', usually in the belief that they are 'landing marks'. The downside of the UFO involvement is the long history of hoaxing, mischief making and the out and out weirdness of the wilder fringes. A further consequence of this is the difficulty in getting the subject taken seriously, a situation which overtook crop circles very early on.

However problematic, the UFO connection is evident from so many accounts of circles, that any attempt to explain the phenomenon must include this. Even the case of the Mowing Devil includes an account of how the farmer's field was 'all aflame' during the night preceding the discovery of the (supposed) crop circle: it is not too fanciful to see in this account some sort of light in the sky. While some writers and observers are prepared to make unequivocal statements to the effect that extra-terrestrial space vehicles are responsible for making circles, it should be remembered that despite thousands of sightings and reports of UFOs, there is still no definitive proof of the extra-terrestrial hypothesis for the origin of UFOs.

If we confine the meaning of the term UFO to its literal sense, as a convenient shorthand for a variety of observations, we can consider this part of the problem without the further complication of hypothetical extra-terrestrial beings. In this context it is possible to interpret UFO sightings as natural events connected to the Earth's geophysical or atmospheric processes. Several writers have suggested that humans in close proximity to UFOs may have their consciousness affected by electromagnetic effects, which could account for the strange accounts of alien encounters or abductions.

What all this means for the circles is a matter of one's own beliefs: as we saw in Chapter 9, explanations about the circles generally say more about individual psychology than anything objective about the actual phenomena. This writer would prefer to understand the association of UFOs with the circles in the context of natural mechanisms. The fact that some individuals are more prone to experience UFO sightings and those cases where adjacent observers are not able to see a UFO, apparently, visible to one of their number, ties in with the reported experiences of the human circlemakers who have had UFO sightings when producing circles. It is their state of a mind, I would contend, that allows or produces such effects.

The meterological ideas which were developed by Dr Meaden have undergone several revisions, the most radical one coming in the wake of the revelations of Doug and Dave. Reflection on the implications of their story led him to virtually abandon the subject, accepting only the simplest events as genuine and consistent with his theory. In this respect he had been forced to accept the criticism made consistently by many other researchers, that many formations showed design complexity that was simply not consistent with a natural force.

Ideas connecting the circles with earth energies remain popular and depend largely on subjective methods, such as dowsing, for validation. As an explanation for the circles, the earth energies approach has been relatively unaffected by the recognition of hoaxing as a major component in the data.

The acknowledgement of the man-made element has been most grudgingly made by the more spiritually inclined researchers, many

of whom see hoaxing in terms of a conspiracy against the circles. Michael Green, one of the founders of the CCCS, who has been at the forefront of the mystical interpreters, has nevertheless gone on record as recognizing that an intelligent evaluation of the subject cannot support a wholesale acceptance of all and any formation as genuine.

To my mind, the most useful approach is one which avoids the either/or thinking of those who insist that only one answer is valid. To the question of who or what causes the circles, the best answer is a composite response, comprising several contradictory ideas: some are man-made, others 'genuine', perhaps due to atmospheric causes, which may include a visible aerial component and could even have interactive properties. While our contemporary worldview may be essentially a scientific one, we need to recognize that many events that we now attach scientific labels to have been observed and known for millennia. They form part of folklore and lie within the realm of poetic imagination, where natural forces were personified, and the intervention of the gods or the spirit world taken for granted.

This model should also include ample recognition of the part that individual and collective psychology plays in the development of the phenomenon, as instigators, observers and operators. There is more than a suggestion that individuals have acted out of motives they do not fully understand, nowhere better illustrated than in Doug and Dave's own mystification at their own behaviour:

> ... when Dave and I have been out in these fields night after night, you can't help wondering about the mystery of the whole universe ... that feeling of mystery, that feeling of why are we here at all. (Doug)

> Doug used to say to me sometimes ... why do we do it ... do you think there's something that makes us? ... We were being told to go out and do them, I know it sounds crazy. (Dave)

Scientific research continues, having promised on several occasions to provide either an answer to the cause of the circles, or a repeatable test for 'genuineness', that would be superior to the human fallibilities of dowsing. It has been observed that when the claims made are fantastic, and the claims of an unknown intelligence are fantastic,

then the demands made of scientific proof need to be high, leaving no room for doubt or error. To date, it does not appear to me that such research has been carried out.

Mysteries remain, epitomized by the enigmatic photograph taken by Busty Taylor in 1994. It showed a lightly imprinted circle with a radial burst pattern which, confident that it was not man-made, he challenged anyone to identify its location. Each new season brings a fresh crop of formations, with no sign of an end, and always the expectation that this year will bring the proof that will support our own particular viewpoint.

At the time of writing there are, as ever, controversies and breaking stories. A video showing some lights apparently creating a pictogram as they move over a field below Oliver's Castle in Wiltshire, has been denounced as a hoax perpetrated with sophisticated video technology. Colin Andrews' website carries a message about a 'major announcement' due shortly, regarding his future plans. Croppies are angry about the NBC film which features John Lundberg creating a pictogram in New Zealand, and a new book by Terry Wilson, *The Secret History of Crop Circles,* detailing many historical cases is due.

PRACTICE

During the season, monitor the press, Internet and television for news of sites to visit. Some research groups operate a 'hot line', which will give updated reports of formations as they occur. Look on the map for ancient sites nearby to reported circles and combine the visit. In the United Kingdom, some well-known sites, such as Avebury, are accessible by public transport. Use your trip to test your own ideas in the field. Talk to other investigators, get the news and gossip!

fURTheR READING AND RESOURCES

This is not intended to be a comprehensive bibliography, but serves as a guide to sources of information on various aspects of the subject.

Books

Crop circles
The first three books published on the circles were:

Andrews, C. and Delgado, P., *Circular Evidence*, Bloomsbury, 1989
Meaden, G. T., *The Circles Effect and its Mysteries*, Artetch/TORRO, 1989
Randles, J. and Fuller, P., *Crop Circles: A Mystery Solved*, Hale, 1990

Although all three books contain material that hindsight shows to be questionable, they remain useful sources and good general introductions.

Bartholomew, A. (ed.), *Harbingers of Change*, Gateway Books, 1991
  A companion volume to Noyes, less factual, more speculative and philosophical.
Collins, A., *The Circle Makers*, ABC Books, 1992
  Looks at the circles in the light of orgone energy and earth mysteries.
Delgado, P. and Andrews, C., *The Latest Evidence*, Bloomsbury, 1990
  Contains good pictures of 1989 and 1990 seasons, but has some very questionable text.
Keen, M., *1991 – Scientific Evidence for the Crop Circle Phenomenon*, Elvery Dowers Publications, 1992
Macnish, J., *Crop Circle Apocalypse*, Circle Vision Publications, 1993
  Shows signs of hasty publication, but contains inside story on Operation Blackbird and his involvement with Doug and Dave.

Meaden, G. T. (ed.), *Circles From the Sky*, Souvenir, 1991
  Summarizes the proceedings of the Oxford Cornference, and
  includes some good eye witness accounts.
Noyes, R. (ed.), *The Crop Circle Enigma*, Photographs by R. Taylor.
  Gateway Books, 1990
  This book was produced by the CCCS and contains essays by
  various writers including John Michell, Terence Meaden, George
  Wingfield and Michael Green.
Schnabel, J., *Round in Circles*, Hamish Hamilton, 1993
  If you only read one other book on the circles, this should be it.

Dowsing
Graves, T., *Dowsing*, Turnstone Press, 1976
Michell, J., (ed.), *Dowsing the Crop Cicles*, Gothic Image Publications,
  1991
Miller, H. and Broadhurst, P., *The Sun and the Serpent*, Pendragon
  Press, 1989
Ozaniec, N., *Dowsing – A Beginner's Guide*, Hodder & Stoughton, 1994
Underwood, G., *The Pattern of the Past*, Museum Press, 1969

General reading
Corliss, W. R., *Handbook of Unusual Natural Phenomena*, Anchor
  Books, 1983
Critchlow, K., *Time Stands Still*, Photographs by R. Bull. Gordon
  Frazer, 1979, and *A Guide to the Stone Circles of Britain, Ireland
  and Brittany*, Yale University Press, 1995
Dames, M., *The Silbury Goddess*, Thames and Hudson, 1976
Dames, M., *The Avebury Cycle*, Thames and Hudson, 1977
Devereux, P., *Earth Lights*, Turnstone Press, 1982
Devereux, P., *Earth Memory*, Quantum, 1991
Devereux, P. and Brookesmith, P., *Fifty Years of Ufology*, Blandford, 1997
Heath, R., *Stone Circles – A Beginner's Guide*, Hodder & Stoughton, 1999
Hyde, M. and McGuiness, M., *Jung for Beginners*, Icon Books, 1992
Meaden, G. T., *The Goddess of the Stones*, Souvenir, 1991
Michell, J., *The New View Over Atlantis*, Thames and Hudson, 1983
Michell, J., *The Dimensions of Paradise*, Thames and Hudson, 1988
Mithen, S., *The Prehistory of the Mind*, Thames and Hudson, 1996
Moorey, T., *Earth Mysteries – A Beginner's Guide*, Hodder & Stoughton,
  1998

JOURNALS

United Kingdom

The Cerealogist is published by Global Circles and edited by John Sayer. It is published three times a year. Cost £10/US $30.
Contact:
J. Sayer
Clements Farm
Wheatley Lane
Kingsley Bordon
Hants
GU 35 3PA

Circular Review is published four times a year. Cost £2.50/US $5.50 per issue.
Contact:
60 Pond View
Moor Lane
Calverton, Nottingham
NG14 6FZ

The Circular is edited by George Bishop and is published quarterly. Cost £4.20/US $5.70 airmail.
Contact:
60 Ramshill Rd
Paignton
Devon
TQ3 3PL

The Spiral is a crop formation newsletter for Wiltshire. Published 11 times a year.
Contact:
The Spiral
27 Silver Birches
All Cannings
Devizes
Wiltshire
SN10 3PA

The Journal of Meteorology is edited by G. T. Meaden. Cost £31 UK; £35 rest of world (surface), £45 (airmail), £22 students/unwaged/senior citizen (UK only). Pay Tornado and Storm Research Organization.
Contact:
Tornado and Storm Research Organisation
QED House
Frome Road
Bradford on Avon
Wiltshire
BA15 1CD

The Crop Watcher is edited by Peter Rendall. Cost £1.50 per issue.
Contact:
Pear Tree Cottage
79 Westerleigh Road
Pucklechurch
Bristol
BS16 9PU

Former editor Paul Fuller can be contacted by e-mail:
100611.1013@compuserve.com

United States

CPRI (Circles Phenomenon Research International)
Newsletter
PO Box 3378
Branford
CT 06405

WEBSITES

Here are a few sites that are worth a visit:

The Crop Circle Connector site is probably the best place to start and
has good links to other pages. It claims 250,000 hits over the last
three years.

The Cerealogist has a site, as does CCCS, CPRI (Colin Andrews'
organization) and Busty Taylor.

CC Research describes itself as 'serious research on crop circles',
and exo Science UFO includes pages on worldwide events. *Circular
Times* is 'oriented towards solutions, truth and pertinent trends of
thought which are positive and uplifting towards human evolution.'

The Circlemakers site is a 'best homepage award winner'.

Dr Meaden's TORRO organization is at **http://www.torro.org.UK/**
and has links to many of the tornado and lightning sites.